MW01095081

Praise for *The Lord's Supper*

"Kleinig cuts through arguments and preconceived beliefs by centering his explanations of the Lord's Supper on Jesus' own words. This book is a must-read for Christians from all faith traditions who want a clear presentation of what Scripture reveals about the great mystery and precious gift of Holy Communion that is Christ himself."

Kelsi Klembara, 1517 Online Content Manager

"Written as only John Kleinig writes, as pastor, as biblical scholar, as simple Christian, this book invites all readers to turn their attention to the texts of Scripture that provide our knowledge of this special gift of Christ, the Supper we call 'the Lord's.' Kleinig draws readers into plumbing the depths of what the Bible says about Christ's meal in the context of meal-taking throughout Scripture. His careful illumination of the four accounts of the Supper in the Gospels and 1 Corinthians draws our attention to oft-overlooked but significant details. Kleinig provides readers with a setting in prayer and simple liturgy for their reading of each chapter, with visual images preceding and hymn verses ending each chapter. This enables readers to focus on what Jesus said about his Supper and how our multimedia communicator God intends us to use and enjoy this feast of forgiveness and new life."

Robert Kolb, professor of systematic theology emeritus,
Concordia Seminary, Saint Louis, Missouri

"The eminent Lutheran theologian John Kleinig is always worth reading, and he has done it again here. Here is food for all Christians, including Roman Catholics such as myself. With scriptural depth and vibrant faith, he calls to mind how much we share in common with respect to the glory of the Lord's Supper, not least in its sacrificial dimension as communion in Christ's body and blood."

Matthew Levering, James N. Jr. and Mary D. Perry Chair
of Theology, Mundelein Seminary

THE LORD'S SUPPER

**See also these titles in the
Christian Essentials Series**

The Apostles' Creed
by Ben Myers

The Lord's Prayer
by Wesley Hill

The Ten Commandments
by Peter J. Leithart

Baptism
by Peter J. Leithart

God's Word
by John W. Kleinig

The Church
by Brad East

THE LORD'S SUPPER

A Guide to the Heavenly Feast

JOHN W. KLEINIG

LEXHAM PRESS

The Lord's Supper: A Guide to the Heavenly Feast
Christian Essentials

Lexham Press, 1313 Commercial St., Bellingham, WA 98225
LexhamPress.com

Print ISBN 9781683597964
Digital ISBN 9781683597971
Library of Congress Control Number 2024939335

Lexham Editorial: Todd Hains, Ethan McCarthy, Paul Robinson, Mandi Newell
Cover Design: Sarah Brossow
Typesetting: Abigail Stocker

24 25 26 27 28 29 30 / IN / 12 11 10 9 8 7 6 5 4 3 2 1

Printed in India

To my dear soul brother and fellow servant of Christ, Dr. Scott Bruzek,
for his faithful stewardship of God's mysteries,
his warm appreciation of the beauty of holiness,
his deep devotion to the regular celebration of the Lord's Supper,
and his fruitful practice of pastoral care that revolves
around Christ's bodily presence there.

CONTENTS

CHRISTIAN ESSENTIALS

SERIES PREFACE

T he Christian Essentials series passes down tradition that matters.

The church has often spoken paradoxically about growth in Christian faith: to grow means to stay at the beginning. The great Reformer Martin Luther exemplified this. "Although I'm indeed an old doctor," he said, "I never move on from the childish doctrine of the Ten Commandments and the Apostles' Creed and the Lord's Prayer. I still daily learn and pray them with my little Hans and my little Lena." He had just as much to learn about the Lord as his children.

The ancient church was founded on basic biblical teachings and practices like the Ten Commandments, baptism, the Apostles' Creed, the Lord's Supper, the Lord's Prayer, and corporate worship. These basics of the Christian life have sustained and nurtured every generation of the faithful—from the apostles to today. They apply equally to old and young, men and women, pastors and church members. "In Christ Jesus you are all sons of God through faith" (Gal 3:26).

We need the wisdom of the communion of saints. They broaden our perspective beyond our current culture and time. "Every age has its own outlook," C. S. Lewis wrote. "It is specially good at seeing certain truths and specially liable to make certain mistakes." By focusing on what's current, we rob ourselves of the insights and questions of those who have gone before us. On the other hand, by reading our forebears in faith, we engage ideas that otherwise might never occur to us.

The books in the Christian Essentials series open up the meaning of the foundations of our faith. These basics are unfolded afresh for today in conversation with the great tradition—grounded in and strengthened by Scripture—for the continuing growth of all the children of God.

> *Hear, O Israel: The Lord our God, the Lord is one. You shall love the Lord your God with all your heart and with all your soul and with all your might. And these words that I command you today shall be on your heart. You shall teach them diligently to your children, and shall talk of them when you sit in your house, and when you walk by the way, and when you lie down, and when you rise. You shall bind them as a sign on your hand, and they shall be as frontlets between your eyes. You shall write them on the doorposts of your house and on your gates. (Deuteronomy 6:4-9)*

PRAYER FOR MEDITATION ON THE LORD'S SUPPER

This order of prayer invites you to read each chapter in the book as a devotional exercise by yourself. It can also be used by a group—with a leader speaking the plain text, and the group speaking the words in bold.

IN GOD'S NAME

In the name of the Father and the Son and the Holy Spirit.
Amen.

O Lord, open my lips
and my mouth will declare your praise.   *Psalm 51:15*
Make haste, O God, to deliver me
make haste to help me, O Lord.   *Psalm 70:1*
Teach me to do your will, for you are my God
Let your good Spirit lead me on a level path.   *Psalm 143:10*

Glory be to the Father and the Son and the Holy Spirit:
as it was in the beginning, is now, and will be forever. Amen.

THE LORD'S SUPPER

INVITATION AND PROMISE

O taste and see that the Lord is good;
happy are those who take refuge in him.   *Psalm 34:8 NRSV*

Jesus says, "Whoever feeds on my flesh and drinks my blood has eternal life, and I will raise him up on the last day."

John 6:54

RESPONSIVE PRAYER

O God, you are my God;
eagerly I seek you.
My soul thirsts for you;
my body longs for you.
Because your love is better than life,
my lips will glorify you.
My soul will be satisfied as with the richest of foods;
with singing lips my mouth
will praise you.   *Psalm 63:1, 3, 5 NIV alt.*
You gave a command to the skies above
and opened the doors of heaven.
You rained down manna for your people to eat.
You gave them the grain of heaven.
They ate the bread of angels;
you sent them all the food they could eat.   *Psalm 78:23–25 NIV alt.*
Blessed is the one you choose and bring near,
to dwell in your courts!

We shall be satisfied with the goodness of your house,
the holiness of your temple!   *Psalm 65:4*
You prepare a table before me
in the presence of my enemies;
you anoint my head with oil;
my cup overflows.
Surely goodness and mercy shall follow me all the days of my life,
and I shall dwell in the house of the LORD forever.   *Psalm 23:5–6*
I will offer to you the sacrifice of thanksgiving
and call on the name of the LORD.   *Psalm 116:17*
O God, you are my God;
eagerly I seek you.
My soul thirsts for you;
my body longs for you.   *Psalm 63:1 NIV alt.*

CLOSING PRAYER

We do not presume to come to this your table, merciful Lord, trusting in our own merits, but in your manifold and great mercies. We are not worthy so much as to gather the crumbs under your table. But you are the same Lord whose nature is always to have mercy. Grant us, therefore, gracious Lord, so to eat the flesh of your dear Son Jesus Christ, and to drink his blood, that our sinful bodies may be made clean by his body, and our souls washed through his precious blood, and that we may evermore dwell in him and he in us.
Amen.

THE LORD'S SUPPER

The poor will eat and be satisfied;
Those who seek the Lord will praise him.   *Psalm 22:26 NIV*

Let us bless the Lord.
Thanks be to God.

The grace of the Lord Jesus Christ and the love of God and the fellowship of the Holy Spirit be with us all.

2 Corinthians 13:14 alt.

Amen.

THE LORD'S SUPPER

We do not presume to come to this your table, merciful Lord, trusting in our own merits, but in your manifold and great mercies.

We are not worthy so much as to gather the crumbs under your table.

But you are the same Lord whose nature is always to have mercy.

Grant us, therefore, gracious Lord,
so to eat the flesh of your dear Son Jesus Christ,
and to drink his blood,

that our sinful bodies may be made clean
by his body, and our souls washed
through his precious blood,

and that we may evermore dwell in him
and he in us. Amen.

WE DO NOT PRESUME TO COME
TO THIS YOUR TABLE, MERCIFUL LORD,
TRUSTING IN OUR OWN MERITS,
BUT IN YOUR MANIFOLD AND
GREAT MERCIES

I

ORIENTATION

He said, "Go into the city to a certain man and say to him,
'The Teacher says, My time is at hand. I will keep
the Passover at your house with my disciples.'"
Matthew 26:18 ESV

This is a handbook on the Lord's Supper. It aims to lead its readers to full participation in the Lord's Supper as a holy meal, a meal that Christ established for the benefit of his disciples in their journey from earth to heaven. It is, if you like, a menu for a lavish, tasty dinner rather than an analysis of its origin, its composition, and the nutritional value of the food it supplies.

Yet even that is a daunting task. While it is, superficially, a simple symbolic meal that consists of a piece of bread and a sip of wine, in reality it is much more than that. In fact most of it is hidden from human sight, such as its location, its host, its guests, and its food. Its location is not just in the place where a congregation of people has assembled, but also in the presence of God in heaven together with all his angels and all the saints who have gone before us. The risen Lord Jesus is its host and God's holy people on earth are its guests. Its food is the body and blood of Jesus.

It is no wonder then that the Lord's Supper has always frustrated all attempts to understand and explain it in rational human terms. It is also no wonder that it has aroused so much disagreement and controversy. It calls into question some of our most widely held assumptions about the nature of the world and our life in it: assumptions about time and space and matter, assumptions about human life and death, as well as our nature and destiny as embodied people. It shows us how limited and one dimensional all these concepts are, and opens us up to appreciate our life on earth as part of a great mystery. Since the Lord's Supper is itself a mystery, we will be able to appreciate it best, and most fully, if we take it as divine banquet that is hosted by the risen Lord Jesus, locate it within the context of God's whole history with his people, and use his word to understand it according to his purpose for it.

T he struggle to understand the Lord's Supper goes back to the difficulty that the disciples of Jesus had in naming it. In fact, even Jesus himself did not give it any name but only told his apostles how to celebrate it, and why. So they, and those who came after them, followed his lead and referred to the whole meal by some part of it. Thus Luke calls it "the breaking of the bread" (Luke 24:35; Acts 2:42). Paul calls it "the Lord's supper" (1 Cor 11:20) and "the table of the Lord" (1 Cor 10:21). By the end of the first century it was called "the Eucharist," or "the Thanksgiving," in an early Christian handbook called the Didache, as well as in the letters of Ignatius.[1] Eventually it was also called "the Sacrament," or "the Blessed Sacrament," or "the Sacrament of the Altar" to indicate that it was a sacred act, and "Holy Communion," a name that recalls Paul's description of it in 1 Corinthians 10:16 as our communal reception of Christ's body and blood and our communion with each other through them.

Since there is no one name for it, I shall use the widely accepted biblical name for it and refer to it as the Lord's Supper. I prefer that name because it reminds us that it is not just an ordinary meal. It is a divine banquet, a festive dinner hosted by the risen Lord Jesus for his disciples.

In Matthew 26:18 Jesus claims that the appointed time for the inauguration of his Supper had come, the time that his heavenly Father had set for it and for his death, a time that coincided with the celebration of that particular Feast of the Passover at that moment in the life of Israel as God's people and the life of Jesus on earth. The Lord's Supper cannot be separated from that context or understood apart from it.

On the one hand, its inauguration comes at the climax of God's dealing with his people. That began with his call of their forefather Abraham, their delivery from slavery in Egypt, and God's covenant with them at Mount Sinai, continued in their life with him in the Promised Land, and culminated in the life and work of Jesus as the promised Messiah. The Lord's Supper marked God's time for a new Passover for all people and a new exodus from death to eternal life with him. Since it is part of that long story it must be understood in the light of all that God did and promised to do then; all the holy meals that God provided for his people in the Old Testament foreshadowed this most holy of all holy meals, just as the earthly service of worship that God instituted for his people at Sinai foreshadowed their participation in the heavenly service of the new covenant with the risen Lord Jesus as its high priest (Heb 10:1).

On the other hand, the Lord's Supper was inaugurated at the climax of the life and work of Jesus by his sacrificial death for all people. It was the hour for the completion of his mission on earth, the mission that his Father sent him to accomplish. We cannot therefore isolate that meal from all the teaching of Jesus about himself and his heavenly Father, his work of helping and healing people in need, and all the other meals that he shared with many different kinds of people. These meals prepare us for that meal; they culminate in his Last Supper with his twelve apostles on the night before his crucifixion (Matt 26:20; Mark 14:17; Luke 22:14) and his meal with two other disciples on the road to Emmaus on the evening of Easter Sunday (Luke 24:28–32).

But the story of the Lord's Supper did not end there. He told the apostles and their successors to celebrate that holy meal regularly and communally with their assembled fellow disciples. Jesus located its subsequent celebration in the life of the church from his resurrection to his reappearance in glory at the end of that age in human history. He continues to host the Lord's Supper for and with his disciples to deliver the benefits of his sacrificial death to them.

I n Acts 2:42 Luke refers to the liturgical context for the celebration of the Lord's Supper after Pentecost by those who had accepted the gospel and had been baptized. He gives us this report about their involvement in common worship: "They devoted themselves to the teaching of the apostles and the common offering, the breaking of the bread and the prayers" (author's translation). These four communal acts are the four main components of the new service of worship in the early church. They describe the congregation's reception of God's word and the Lord's Supper and its consequent reaction to receiving them. Thus "the teaching of the apostles" is coupled with "the communal offering," and "the breaking of the bread" is coupled with "the prayers." Each of these is qualified by a definite article to show that they are familiar, technical terms which do not require any further explanation by Luke for his readers.

The first of these communal acts was the teaching of the apostles. This term includes two things—the reading of selected passages from the Old Testament and their use of them to teach the gospel of Jesus as the crucified and risen Christ (Luke 24:27, 44–47). Readings from the Gospels and the Epistles were later added to the readings from the Old Testament in what was later called "the service of the word."

The second communal act, which was associated with the proclamation of God's word by the apostles, is usually translated as "fellowship."[2] In Greek it describes a common possession, a common relationship, or, as in this case, a common act. In this context it most likely describes the presentation of a common offering. That is how it is used elsewhere in some passages in the New Testament (2 Cor 8:4; 9:13; Heb 13:16).[3] Thus in 2 Corinthians 9:13 Paul commends the members of the congregation in Corinth for the generosity of their "contribution," their common offering for the relief of impoverished Christians in Jerusalem. This interpretation is supported by the subsequent note in Acts 2:44 that all the believers had all things "in common."

The third communal act was "the breaking of the bread." For Luke this was the technical term for the communal celebration of the Lord's Supper as a unique sacrificial meal (Luke 24:35; Acts 2:42; 20:7). This name for that meal recalls what Jesus did when he instituted the Sacrament (Matt 26:26; Mark 14:22; Luke 22:19; 1 Cor 11:24), and how he is still present at every celebration of this meal as its unseen host (Luke 24:30). Taken together with "the teaching of the apostles," it recalls

Luke's description in 24:13–35 of the disclosure of the risen Lord Jesus to the two disciples on the evening of Easter Sunday in two stages, first by his proclamation of himself from the Old Testament, and then by acting as their host at their evening meal.

The fourth communal act was the devotion of the congregation to "the prayers," which flowed from "the breaking of the bread" and was associated with it. The use of the rather unusual plural indicates that this does not just refer to a single prayer but alludes to the full range of corporate prayers.[4] It includes the Lord's Prayer and other liturgical prayers such as Maranatha (which means "Our Lord, come," from 1 Cor 16:22), the chanting of psalms and the singing of hymns, as well as intercessory prayer for the church in all places, all people, and even the enemies of the church (1 Tim 2:1–6). So from its very beginning the mother congregation in Jerusalem devoted itself to common prayer in their common worship in response to Christ's offering of his body and blood to them.

The risen Lord Jesus continues his ministry in word and deed through the service of worship. There he continues to host his Holy Supper. Each of the other three parts of the service contribute to our full participation in it. Both the Old Testament and the stories of Jesus tell us what he is doing for us and giving to us in the Lord's Supper. The prayers aid our faithful response to the gospel of Jesus, and the offering of gifts is the appropriate response to Christ's self-giving to us in the Supper.

Since the Lord's Supper has been established by Jesus, who now presides over it as its host, we depend on him for our instruction in it. He does that in the New Testament by the four reports of its institution in Matthew 26:26–29, Mark 14:22–25, Luke 22:14–30, and 1 Corinthians 11:23–26, as well as his teaching about it in John 6. Through these passages he himself instructs us in what he does and what we receive from him in the Lord's Supper.

I n what follows, I will not adopt an apologetic, defensive stance in an attempt to justify the traditional teaching of the church on the Lord's Supper, or even my own beliefs as a Lutheran pastor. Nor will I take a polemical, offensive stance in an attempt to refute false teaching and wrong practices of the Supper. I will not deal with it academically by exploring its possible human origin or its complex human development in the history of the church. Nor will I use the resources of philosophy to explain its paradoxes, such as whether and how Christ can be present with his humanity both in heaven and on earth, or whether and how the bread and wine can be the body and blood of Jesus. Rather, I shall invite you to attend to what Jesus himself has to say about his Supper. Thus my approach to this topic will be scriptural and personal and practical.

This best suits our study of the Lord's Supper because it is such a great mystery. All too often people confuse a mystery with a secret because they both have to do with what is hidden and unknown. But a mystery differs from a secret in one decisive respect. A secret comes from ignorance and inexperience, the lack of information about something or our inadequate understanding of it. A secret ceases to be a secret once you know it. But a mystery remains hidden even when you know it. In fact, it becomes more mysterious and wonderful the more you know it. Take the mystery of human love, and the souls of the people that we love. Both are ultimately unfathomable. The more we know them, the more we realize that we do not know them and can never know them fully at all; we realize how little we know them and how limited our knowledge of them is. What's more, what we do know depends on continual interaction and ongoing conversation with them. That is also true for the mystery of Jesus and his Holy Supper. And even more so because this is a divine, heavenly mystery.

I am well aware that even the most eloquent and passionate written prose fails to communicate the wonder of the Lord's Supper. That is done best by an attitude of reverent devotion and astonished adoration. While prayer and praise fit us well for the proper appreciation of a divine mystery, sung poetry enables us to express what we otherwise find so hard to teach, let alone explain. It helps us to contemplate and adore what we can never fully fathom. So I shall end each part of this handbook with a stanza or stanzas of hymns that do this well.

My approach to the Lord's Supper in this handbook is best described by Paul in his teaching on the presence of the risen Lord Jesus in the church in Colossians 1:25–27: "I became a minister according to the stewardship from God that was given to me for you, to make the word of God fully known, the mystery hidden for ages and generations but now revealed to his saints. To them God chose to make known how great among the gentiles are the riches of the glory of this mystery, which is Christ in you, the hope of glory." Paul uses God's word to lead God's holy people ever further and deeper into the mystery of Christ's presence among them in the church on earth—his hidden presence which provides them with a foretaste of their glory in heaven. That is what I would like to do with you as we explore the mystery of the Lord's Supper together.

> Your body and Your blood,
> Once slain and shed for me,
> Are taken at your table, Lord,
> In blest reality.
>
> Search not how this takes place,
> This wondrous mystery;
> God can accomplish vastly more
> Than what we think could be.

> "Your Table I Approach," verses 3–4 (alt.)
> Gerhard Wolter Molanus[5]

II

THE MEAL OF MEALS

People will come from east and west, and from north and south,
and recline at table in the kingdom of God.
Luke 13:29 ESV

eals matter much more than we usually realize. They matter, in part, because they provide us with the physical nourishment we need to survive and thrive. Yet we don't need to have meals to do that. Like the animals we could gain food from snacking, or just eating by ourselves whenever we were hungry. But a meal is much more than that.

We get an inkling of this from those tribal people who are hunters and gatherers. They do not eat their food by themselves; they share the meat they have hunted and the foodstuff they have gathered. What's more, they don't eat it raw, but prepare it for better nourishment, and then share what they have prepared with each other in a communal meal. The same food is eaten by all the members of their tribal family and its guests.

Meals are social acts, communal enactments, human rituals that distinguish us from the animals. We receive much more from them than mere physical nourishment. They socialize and humanize us. They order our lives physically, personally, socially, and spiritually with our location in time and space, society, and community. They establish us as people in the communities that both support us and affirm our personal status.

Since ancient times meals have had some distinctive traits that are still evident today. In most cases they are family gatherings. In them the members of a family gather at home with each other around a table. Meals can at times be located in another place, such as a restaurant, and include other guests as honorary members of the family. They can also occur in gatherings of other communities, such as clubs or meetings of people engaged in a common enterprise. But their proper place is with families. They are an essential part of family life—part of what holds a family together and ensures that it functions properly.

Family meals recur at certain set times of the day, whether in the morning, at midday, or, most commonly, in the evening. They also occur at other significant, festive times for the family, such as anniversaries, like birthdays, or on religious occasions, like Sundays or Easter or Christmas. They often celebrate major social events, like weddings, and religious events, like baptisms.

The most significant of these are feasts that celebrate a significant occasion with the very best food and drink. They are times for jubilation that may be enhanced by speeches and toasts, singing, music making, and dancing. All these meals synchronize the lives of people in families and communities.

Meals unfold in a set order with a repeated sequence of courses. The host of the meal determines when it begins and when it ends. The menu may vary but the courses usually follow the same set pattern. In my family, the meal revolves around a main course of meat, vegetables, and potatoes or rice. Before the main course is served there may be a light preparatory course with an appetizer or some soup. After the main course there may be a dessert of fruit or a pudding or something baked. In keeping with the occasion, dessert may be more elaborate.

Most significantly, shared meals are social events in which all participants share in the same food, enjoy the same status despite all their differences, and engage in an open conversation with each other as listeners and speakers. By sharing a meal they all have communion with each other and so grow together in community. To facilitate that communal interaction and consolidation, their behavior is governed by a code of table manners and the proper etiquette for the occasion. Shared meals put everyone on the same footing, as people whose identity and worth is given by their place in family and community.

Such meals teach a great deal in a very practical way. What's more, this happens discreetly, so that those who participate are mostly unaware of what is being taught and learned. That applies especially for family meals. In them its members learn to share and care for each other. They learn to give and receive. They learn what a happy life in a family offers and what it requires. Through them parents learn to show consideration and love for their children, while children learn to honor and love their parents. Through its meals the social and religious heritage of the family is taught and caught.

All this combines to ensure that a meal accomplishes much more than the mere provision of physical nourishment. The sharing of the same food establishes and maintains a community of people who have more in common than just food, such as friendship with each other or the same religious affiliation. It incorporates new people into a community by the hospitality that it offers and restores those who have previously been sidelined or excluded from it. It honors people and affirms their status, whether it be their newly conferred status, such as a daughter-in-law or son-in-law in a wedding banquet, or their prior status, such as friends or relatives who have been invited to a dinner. Above all, the sharing of food in a meal demonstrates and enacts personal acceptance and approval, love and affection. Participation in a common meal is, at best, the way people give of themselves and honor each other.

With all this in mind, we should not be surprised by the significance of meals in the Bible. The Bible begins with God's provision of grain from plants and fruit from trees for Adam and Eve (Gen 1:29), and of meat from animals for Noah and his descendants (Gen 9:2–3). It ends with God's invitation to participate in the eternal marriage supper that celebrates the union of Jesus with his bride (Rev 19:9), and his congratulation of those who are given the right to eat the fruit from the previously forbidden tree of life (Rev 22:14). In between, there are many festive meals God hosts for his people, meals that become more remarkable with the passage of time.

The first communal meal God provided for his people was the feast of the Passover in Egypt (Exod 12:1–28). It was a sacrificial meal in which God's people ate the meat from a male lamb or goat and unleavened bread with their families in their homes on the night before their deliverance from slavery, and then each year, first at the tabernacle and later at the temple, to commemorate that event. This was later matched by God's miraculous, regular provision of bread from heaven for his people in the desert (Exod 16; see also Ps 78:17–25).

God, the heavenly King, also hosted a unique sacrificial meal for the leaders of Israel at Mount Sinai, to ratify his covenant with them and sanctify them as his holy people with the blood of the covenant (Exod 24:1–11). On this occasion these leaders saw God on the mountain and ate and drank in his presence. This holy banquet was depicted as his royal audience with his courtiers, like Solomon with his servants (1 Kgs 3:15).

These meals culminated in the holy meals God instituted for his people through Moses. By the offerings they presented to him he fed them with holy food in the divine service of worship, first at the tabernacle and then at the temple. These holy meals were envisaged as royal meals in which the divine King sat at table in his house with his servants each morning and evening, and invited his citizens to holy festive meals that he spread for them three times a year (1 Kgs 4:27; 10:5). There God gave back a portion of the foodstuff that was offered to him. On one hand, he gave his servants, the priests, some of the most holy meat from the sin offerings (Lev 6:24–26, 29) and guilt offerings of the people (Lev 7:6), and some of the most holy bread from the grain offerings (Lev 2:3, 10; 6:14–17) and the showbread (Lev 24:5–7). This foodstuff was called "divine bread," or "the bread of God" (Lev 21:6, 8; 22:25). They ate this most holy food from the Lord's table in his presence at the sanctuary.[6] On the other hand, he also provided his people with most of the leftover holy meat and bread that they brought as fellowship offerings and tithes to him on the three great pilgrim festivals, the feasts of Passover, Pentecost, and Booths (Lev 7:11–18; Deut 12:17–18; 15:19–20; 16:16–17). In these festive meals they ate and rejoiced in the Lord's presence with their families as his honored guests (Deut 12:18–19; 14:23; 15:20).

The focus on meals is even sharper and clearer in the ministry of Jesus in the New Testament. All that Jesus says and does is connected with meals. His obvious enjoyment of them earned him the reputation of a glutton and drunkard (Matt 11:19; Luke 7:34). Luke reports how Jesus participated in meals as a guest (5:29–32; 7:36–50; 19:1–10), or the host (9:10–17), or both guest and host (22:14–30). He tells us that Jesus described his proclamation of the gospel as an invitation to a royal banquet (14:7–24) and depicted his future care for his faithful disciples as both the host and the waiter in the banquet that he would provide for them (12:37; 22:24–30).

We see the same association of the mission of Jesus with meals in John's Gospel. There the first of seven miracles that Jesus performed as signs of his divine status and mission was the transformation of water into wine at the wedding feast in Cana, even though he was present only a guest (John 2:1–11).[7] John's fourth sign was the feeding of five thousand people with five small loaves and two tiny fish (6:1–14), which introduced his discourse on himself as the bread of life (6:22–71). After his performance of the seventh sign, the raising of Lazarus, Jesus was the guest of honor at a meal with Lazarus, in which Martha waited on him and Mary anointed his feet with expensive perfume in preparation for his death and burial (12:1–8). In John chapters 13–17 all Jesus's previous discourses culminated in a farewell discourse with his disciples and his prayer of consecration during his Passover supper with them. In his final story, John reports how the risen Lord Jesus revealed himself to seven of his disciples and provided a breakfast of fish and bread for them (21:1–14).

Just as all the Gospels show how the mission of Jesus culminated in his death and resurrection, so the purpose of all the meals in which Jesus was present as a guest or host is fulfilled and disclosed by the celebration of his final Passover with his disciples on the night before his death. There he instituted a new meal for them (Matt 26:17–29; Mark 14:12–25; Luke 22:14–23). It was a strange meal, in which he gave them his body to eat and his blood to drink—a sacrificial meal in which he disclosed the purpose of his unjust execution as a sin offering for them. This was not just another meal in a long line of holy meals. It was the meal of meals, the feast to end all feasts. Jesus did not establish it as an optional celebration; he commanded his disciples to continue to celebrate it in remembrance of him.

What a far-reaching meal it is! It reaches back to the fruit from the tree of life that God withheld from our first human parents in the Garden of Eden, as well as the holy food he gave to his people in the Old Testament as a foretaste of the feast to come. Through the incarnation and exaltation of Jesus it is a heavenly meal that reaches down from heaven to people on earth, and takes them up into heaven from earth (John 6:50, 58). Through his ministers it reaches out to people from all nations around the world (Luke 14:15–24). It reaches forward from the death of Jesus to the end of human history by its anticipation of the resurrection of the body and eternal life with God (1 Cor 11:26). But most of all, the meal itself is the new testament by which Jesus conveys all that he has to us as his heirs (1 Cor 11:25). In it he offers himself to us and shares all that he has gained for us by his human life, unjust death, and bodily resurrection.

All this is such a rich cornucopia of abundant blessing that we cannot fully grasp it, let alone exhaust its bounty. It comes to us as a free gift from Jesus, a legacy we receive by faith in him and in what he has promised to give to us and to all his guests.

I n this little book I would like to whet your appetite for that meal of meals by telling you what God himself teaches us about it in the Bible. Yet that is a rather presumptuous undertaking, because I can't really do that for you with my limited imagination and even more limited powers of persuasion. Only Jesus himself can show that to you by your own participation in his Holy Supper, like the two disciples at Emmaus, whose eyes were opened by the risen Lord Jesus when he broke bread with them (Luke 24:30–35). There, in the meal that he hosts for you, you too will recognize him who is otherwise unseeable and unseen.

> We have no need to go to heaven
> To bring our long-sought Savior down;
> You are to all already given,
> And even now our banquet crown.
> To every faithful soul appear,
> And show your very presence here.

> "Victim Divine, Your Grace We Claim," verse 3 (alt.)
> Charles Wesley[8]

WE ARE NOT WORTHY
SO MUCH AS TO GATHER THE CRUMBS
UNDER YOUR TABLE

III

THE FEAST WITHIN A FEAST

*And he said to them, "I have eagerly desired
to eat this Passover with you before I suffer."*
Luke 22:15 NIV

Jesus provides us with a strange meal in his Holy Supper, a new meal unlike any other in the Bible, let alone in human history. Its strangeness can distract and bamboozle us so completely that we get lost in a mental maze as we try to understand it intellectually and make sense of it theologically.

But Luke shifts our attention away from explaining the meaning and purpose of the meal to the personal, emotional reason Jesus gives for its institution. Luke does this by introducing his account of its inauguration with a report about how much Jesus had longed to celebrate this Passover meal with his disciples (22:15). In the first of the seven discourses that relate what Jesus said that evening[9] he expressed his passionate desire to eat it with them before he suffered and died. So the first thing that Jesus wants his disciples to know about that meal is his long-standing, ardent longing to share it with them.

Luke is the only Evangelist who reports these warm words of Jesus. They are without parallel in all the other teaching of Jesus. The closest statement to it comes from John 13:1, where John introduces his account of the Last Supper with John's declaration that Jesus not only loved his disciples while he was with them in the world, but that he loved them to the end, utterly and completely, without reservation and qualification. Here in Luke 22:15, however, Jesus himself opens his heart to them. He shows how his association with them culminates in his celebration of this last Passover meal with them. This was what he longed for most of all over the three years that he had spent with them.

The desire of Jesus to eat this Passover with them was not just a passing whim, a transient fancy. He had kept on yearning and longing to eat this meal with them for a long time, like a father for the birth of his child, or an engaged woman for her marriage. This, he implies, was what motivated him from the beginning of his ministry to this hour. He also implies that he had planned it carefully and deliberately, with all its details, so that it would accomplish all that he wanted at its inauguration and by its subsequent celebration.

But why did he so eagerly desire to eat this Passover meal with them? He had, it seems, shared many other meals with them, including Passover meals. But this one was different. It was not just different because it was his last meal with them before his death; it was different because in it he gave them a new meal, a meal within that wonderful festive meal, a meal that superseded all the other holy meals of the old covenant. It was the meal of the new covenant in his blood (Luke 22:20).

I n his account, Luke tells us four things about this new meal. He tells us how it differed from the Passover, what kind of meal it was, how it was to be repeated, and what its guests received from Jesus in it.

First, even though it was embedded in a Passover meal and had some things in common with it, this new meal differed quite sharply from the Passover. It differed in its menu and its beneficiaries. For one thing, there was no meat from a lamb or kid to eat. To be sure there was bread to eat and wine to drink, as was the case in every Passover banquet. But in this new meal Jesus himself took the place of the Passover lamb, and gave his disciples his own body to eat in the bread and his own blood to drink in the wine. Jesus also distinguished his role as the meal's host from the role of his disciples as his guests (Luke 22:16, 18).

Even though he seems to have eaten some of the Passover lamb and drunk some of the Passover wine on that occasion (Matt 26:17; Mark 14:12, 14; Luke 22:8, 11, 15), he had nothing to eat and nothing to drink in that new meal that he was instituting, either initially or subsequently. He declared, most emphatically, that he would no longer eat or drink with them in that meal. They alone would eat and drink in his presence.

In contrast with the hosts of normal social and religious meals, he himself would not enjoy the food and drink that he provided for them. The meal was for their benefit only.

Yet that would not always be so. His self-imposed ban was an interim measure. It would last from his death until the end of the present age, with the coming of God's heavenly kingdom and its fulfillment in the age to come (Luke 22:16, 18). His Holy Supper therefore partly anticipated the eternal heavenly feast, the marriage supper of the Lamb (Rev 19:9), just as an engagement party anticipates a marriage feast.

Second, the Passover banquet was a family meal, in which the father as its head hosted the meal for the members of his extended family and other invited guests. But this new celebration was a collegial meal provided by Jesus for his disciples, like a wisdom teacher for his students (Prov 9:1–5), or even like Solomon as the wise teacher of his courtiers (1 Kgs 3:15). Jesus was the host of this new meal in his capacity as a royal teacher (Luke 22:11, 25–30). As the teacher of his disciples Jesus hosted an unusual kind of "educational" meal in the heart of the Passover, a ritual meal by which he taught them by what he gave of himself to them in it.

In chapters 13–17 of his Gospel, John shows us that this Passover celebration was an occasion in which Jesus taught his disciples about himself and his heavenly Father. But that is not Luke's emphasis. In Luke's telling, Jesus did not offer that kind of cognitive theological instruction. Nevertheless, it was still meant to teach them his most important lesson. In it he did not teach *about* himself in an intellectual, didactic way; he actually taught *himself* to them, personally and practically.

And he ensured that he would be able to do so even after his death. That, in fact, was his intention in that celebration. Like a master craftsman with his apprentices, he taught them by doing. He taught them by what he did as well as by what he said as he did it. He taught himself to them by hosting a new meal, in which he gave them his body to eat and his blood to drink. He also taught them by telling them what he was giving to them, and by instructing them to do and say what he had done in remembrance of him. So he himself was both the teacher and the lesson, an unusual lesson that was not learned by the application of intelligence and mental aptitude, but was learned, like the love of a person, by hearing what he was saying and receiving what he was giving. It was not just one of many lessons. It was an unending, inexhaustible, summative lesson, because in it he gave himself and all that he had to his disciples as they were ready to receive it.

Third, Jesus made it quite clear that his disciples were to repeat the meal after that occasion. Right at its beginning he told them to "do" what he was doing (Luke 22:19). He did not tell them to repeat the Passover meal ever again, but he did authorize and commission them to repeat the new meal of the new covenant in his blood. Just as Jesus did not celebrate his final Passover with all his disciples, but only with the twelve apostles he had chosen to act on his behalf and represent him (Luke 6:12–16), so he commissioned them to host this new meal in the future on his behalf as his agents by telling them to perform it in remembrance of him (Luke 22:19). We can surmise from his declaration that he would be among them in their ministry (Luke 22:27), and they would preside over the meal together with him, as its unseen host. That would be their task, their responsibility as his apostles.

What's more, since the Lord's Supper was meant to be repeated in the future, he also, by implication, commissioned their successors in ministry to host the meal when the apostles could not do so and after they had died. Like the apostles, they would share the royal authority of Jesus, the authority he had received from his heavenly Father (Luke 22:29). As the teachers of God's new people they would eat and drink at his table and sit as royal teachers on thrones together with him (Luke 22:30).[10] The meal by which Jesus inaugurated his Holy Supper in anticipation of his death also anticipated the meal's actual celebration after his death and resurrection.

Fourth, in this meal Jesus gave his disciples something completely new, something that no one had ever done before. By that meal he made a new covenant with them, a new covenant in his blood (Luke 22:20), a covenant that surpassed God's covenant with them at Mount Sinai, which had been made with the blood of young bulls (Exod 24:1–12). This new meal was not just the last will and testament, ratified for them on the night before his death; it also conveyed his full legacy to them, and through them to the whole world. Through it he wanted to share with them everything that he had gained by his holy life and his sacrificial death. Through it he gave them a fore-taste of all that they would receive from him by sharing in his death, resurrection, and exaltation. It is no wonder that Jesus passionately desired to eat that last Passover meal with them.

The ardent desire of Jesus to share the new meal of the covenant in his blood with his disciples challenges us to match his desire for us with our own desire to receive it. The meal is meant to awaken and increase our longing for it. It is meant to arouse our hunger and thirst for it and enhance our wholehearted enjoyment of it. By his fervent desire and ardent love for us he woos us and sues for the same from us; he solicits and elicits our love. And best of all, he promises that those who come to him will be so satisfied that they will never hunger and thirst for anything else (John 6:35).

> Ah, how hungers all my spirit
> For the love I do not merit!
> Oft have I, with sighs fast thronging,
> Thought upon this food with longing,
> In the battle well-nigh worsted,
> For this cup of life have thirsted,
> For the Friend who here invites me
> And to God Himself unites me.
>
> "Soul, Adorn Thyself with Gladness," verse 4 (alt.)
> Johann Franck[11]

IV

AN ORDERED MEAL

For I received from the Lord what I also delivered to you.
1 Corinthians 11:23 NIV

The Lord's Supper is, by any reckoning, an unusual meal. From a human point of view, it is not really a proper meal at all. It is a meager meal in which a group of people, large or small, eat a bit of bread and drink a sip of wine. It is offered by an invisible host who is represented by a visible person who acts as his proxy. In it that unseen host claims to give his body to eat and his blood to drink. Yet there is no visible evidence of that at all. At best this celebration seems to portray a charade of a meal rather than an actual meal.

Yet for those who appreciate its bounty, it is the meal of meals, a feast that outdoes all other feasts. In religious terms it even surpasses the great Passover Feast that provided the context for its inauguration. It is a supernatural feast that grants people on earth a foretaste of life in heaven. Even though it seems plain and insignificant, it is utterly extraordinary, mysterious, and wonderful, because all its bounty is hidden from human sight behind and beyond its unremarkable appearance.

It is remarkable because it is not a human invention, even though it seems to be nothing more than a customary, human celebration. It is, instead, a divine ordinance, a supernatural ceremonial meal that Jesus ordained for his disciples and provided for them as God's Son. He is its original founder and its ongoing host. He determines what happens in it and offers what is received from him in it. By what he did and said at its inauguration on the night before his death he made it the meal of all meals, a holy, heavenly meal for his guests.

There are four accounts of the meal's foundation (Matt 26:26–29; Mark 14:22–25; Luke 22:19–20; 1 Cor 11:23–25). It is therefore well-attested biblically. It is also well-attested historically, because Paul's report of its origin is part of the oral instruction he received at his conversion in AD 33, three years after the death of Jesus, and recorded in writing in his first letter to the Christians in Corinth around AD 56 or 57. Those accounts give us a clear outline of what Jesus did and said when he established his Holy Supper.

The sequence of events is quite clear and certain despite minor differences in emphasis and expression, largely due to the translation of the original record of it in Aramaic into the

Greek texts we have in the New Testament. Table 1 on the following page shows us what Jesus did on that occasion.[12]

Each of these accounts reports the two main parts of the meal in a single sentence. The three Gospels have the same sequence of acts in which each writer highlights the most important acts by the use of a main verb rather than a participle.

Jesus does five things with the bread as the host of the meal. He takes it, blesses it, breaks it, gives it to his disciples, and tells his guests what it is. Similarly Jesus does four things with the cup of wine. He takes it, gives thanks for it, gives it to his disciples, and tells them what it is. For both the bread and the wine, the emphasis is on the prayer of blessing or thanksgiving, the bestowal of bread or wine, and the words that accompany their bestowal.

Paul's abbreviated account omits some details as unnecessary for his teaching. He does not tell us that Jesus gave the bread to his disciples, took the cup of wine, gave thanks for it, and gave it to his disciples. He assumes that the people in Corinth are familiar with all this from their participation in the Lord's Supper. Paul's emphasis is on what Jesus said about the bread and the cup of wine as the heart of the meal and its significance for them.

E ven though there are no significant differences between the four accounts about what Jesus did when he inaugurated his Holy Supper, they do differ from each other in their report of what Jesus said. This is evident in the data summarized in table 2.

MATTHEW 26:26–27	MARK 14:22–24
Taking bread,	**Taking** bread,
and blessing,	blessing,
Jesus **broke**	he **broke**
and giving it to his disciples	and **gave** it to them
he **said**	and **said**
Taking the cup	Taking the cup,
and giving thanks,	giving thanks,
he **gave** it to them,	he **gave** it to them, and they all drank from it,
saying	and he **said** to them

LUKE 22:19–20	1 CORINTHIANS 11:23–25
Taking bread,	The Lord Jesus Christ **took** bread
giving thanks,	and, giving thanks,
he **broke**	he **broke**
and **gave** it to them,	
saying	and **said**
And likewise the cup after they had eaten,	And likewise the cup after they had eaten,
saying	saying

MATTHEW 26:26, 27–28	MARK 14:22, 24
Take!	Take!
Eat!	
This is my body.	This is my body
Drink of it, all of you!	
This is my blood of the covenant,	This is my blood of the new covenant,
poured out for many for the forgiveness of sins.	poured out on behalf of many.

LUKE 22:19–20	1 CORINTHIANS 11:24–25
This is my body, given on behalf of you.	This is my body, which is given on behalf of you.
Do this in remembrance of me.	Do this in remembrance of me.
This cup is the new covenant in my blood,	This cup is the new covenant in my blood.
poured out on your behalf.	
	Do this, whenever you drink it, in remembrance of me.

The words of Jesus that accompany his actions are what linguists call "speech acts." Speech acts are words that either instruct people to do something (like when I tell someone to shut the door) or accomplish something by being spoken (like parents who name their child, or a celebrant who marries a couple).

On one hand, we have two sets of ritual instructions. Jesus tells his apostles to take the bread that he gives as a gift to them (Matt 26:26; Mark 14:22) and eat it (Matt 26:26). He also commissions them to host the same meal on future occasions (Luke 22:19; 1 Cor 11:24). Likewise he tells all of them to drink the wine from the cup (Matt 26:27) and commissions them to offer it to others as well (1 Cor 11:25).

On the other hand, we also have Jesus's performative sayings, by which he presents his gifts to his guests and tells them what kind of gifts they are, like when I present a wrapped-up birthday present to my wife and wish her a happy birthday verbally or by what I write in a card that I give together with it. On this occasion Jesus presents some bread and a cup of wine to his guests and tells them that the bread is his body and the wine is his blood. He also tells them why it was given, like when I present some flowers as a spontaneous gift to my wife to show her that I love her and thank her for her love. Thus he tells his guests that the blood which had been shed as a sacrificial offering on their behalf is now offered to them for their benefit. The formula that Jesus uses for his gift of a cup with wine is much more complex. By giving them the wine he gives them his blood, the blood by which he makes a new covenant with them. He also declares that the wine he now pours out for them and that he will pour for them is the blood that he poured out as a sacrifice for them. He gives them his blood so that they can receive divine pardon, the forgiveness of sins. So the words of Jesus are the key to his acts, which accomplish little or nothing for us apart from the words. The words not only interpret what he does, but actually offer what Jesus provides for us in his meal. They show us what we cannot see. They disclose the hidden side of this lavish feast for us. Even though it is not at all lavish in its provision of physical bread and wine, it is utterly lavish in the invisible food that it offers and its invisible benefits.

T he four accounts that we have in the New Testament do not describe everything Jesus did at the Last Supper, nor do they prescribe everything that had to be done whenever the Lord's Supper would subsequently be celebrated. Rather, they give us an outline of what Jesus said and did to present us with his mandate for its future celebration. They tell us what he prescribed as necessary for its valid enactment as his supper. The apostles and their successors were to take bread and wine, bless or thank God for them, present them to Christ's disciples as his guests, and repeat the words that Jesus had spoken over the bread and the wine.

We are not told exactly what Jesus said before he offered the bread and wine to his disciples. Matthew and Mark tell us that Jesus "blessed" the bread. That was the normal practice for every Jewish meal. The head of the family would begin the meal with a "blessing," an act of praise by which he acknowledged the Lord as the giver of all that they were to eat in the meal as God had commanded them to do (Deut 8:10). The stock formula to begin such an act of praise was, "Blessed are you, Lord God," before the reason for it was given, which could then also introduce a petitionary prayer. That was and still is the normal pattern for prayer for Jewish people. Thus the usual prayer before the meal is: "Blessed are you, Lord God, the King of the Universe, who brings forth bread from the earth." By their recitation of that blessing, with its invocation of God's holy name, the meal is sanctified, becoming a holy meal eaten in God's presence.

Since Luke and Paul were addressing a gentile audience that was unfamiliar with this entrenched Jewish practice and the Hebrew way of thinking in it, they translated this term by speaking about "giving thanks" to God for the food that they were about to eat. That is also the term for the prayer over the wine in all four accounts. By giving thanks to God the Father, Jesus acknowledged that the whole meal was God's good gift to them. As the host of this new meal, he thanked God for his generous provision.

This set the precedent for what was to be done by the apostles and their successors when they presided over each subsequent celebration of the Lord's Supper. They would consecrate the bread and wine as Christ's body and blood by recalling what Jesus had said and done with a prayer of thanksgiving for what was given by him, for as Paul teaches, all the food that came from God was consecrated by the word of God and prayer and received with thanksgiving (1 Tim 4:4–5).

The order of the Lord's Supper with the arrangement of its parts determines its purpose and our understanding of it. It shows us what Jesus meant to accomplish in it, and why. It shows us what Jesus gave to his disciples to eat and drink, and how it was meant to benefit them. The four New Testament reports of its main parts all culminate in the words of Jesus, because they give us the key to its purpose.

The main features of the new festive meal that Jesus established for his disciples stand out vividly by comparison with the order and arrangement of the Passover meal. Jesus himself hosts the Lord's Supper for his disciples rather than the head of the family for his household and its guests. The body of Jesus replaces the meat from the Passover lamb. In the Lord's Supper there is only one cup of wine, rather than the four cups that were distributed at the Passover. In the Lord's Supper, the cup of wine was circulated so that all the guests would drink from the same cup, instead of pouring some of it into their own cups, as was the usual practice. Even though Jesus told all his disciples to drink from his cup, he himself did not drink of it. Unlike the blood of the Passover lamb, which could not be consumed but had to be poured out on the altar of the temple or daubed on the doorposts of their houses, the blood of Jesus was given for them to drink in the cup with its wine. The wine itself was the blood of Jesus, the blood of his new covenant with them. All of this shows that the Lord's Supper is a gift given for the disciples' benefit, nourishment, and replenishment.

A t the end of Matthew's Gospel the risen Lord Jesus commissions his eleven apostles to teach his disciples to observe all that he had commanded them (Matt 28:19–20). That mandate includes the celebration of his Holy Supper. He commanded them to host that holy meal and eat the food and drink the drink he gave to them and to all his disciples in it. He ordered its celebration and arranged how it was to be celebrated so that he could offer them that food and that drink. They did not arrange it for themselves; he arranged it for them so that he could accomplish his purpose for them by their participation in it.

This is the hour of banquet and of song;
This is the heav'nly table spread for me;
Here let me feast and, feasting, still prolong
The brief bright hour of fellowship with Thee.

Feast after feast thus comes and passes by,
Yet, passing, points to that glad feast above,
Giving sweet foretaste of the festal joy,
The Lamb's great marriage feast of bliss and love.

"Here, O My Lord, I See Thee Face to Face," verses 3 and 7
Horatius Bonar[13]

BUT YOU ARE THE SAME LORD WHOSE NATURE IS ALWAYS TO HAVE MERCY

V

A SACRIFICIAL BANQUET

Christ, our Passover Lamb has been sacrificed. Let us therefore celebrate the festival, not with the old leaven, the leaven of malice and evil, but with the unleavened bread of sincerity and truth.
1 Corinthians 5:7–8 ESV

There is much that is odd, if not uncanny, in what Jesus does in his Supper and says about what he is doing. His words about the bread as his body and the wine as his blood are, on any account, strange. They puzzle and mystify us. While some people are understandably horrified and shocked by them, I, like many others, am fascinated by them and drawn to them. I am challenged by them because they are so incredible, and attracted to them because they are so wonderful; indeed they seem too good to be true. But since Jesus said them, they must be true.

By themselves his words are quite clear and plain. What they refer to is also clear. We all know what bread and wine are. So too the body and blood of a person. Yet it is difficult to fathom how they are related. It is even more difficult to fathom how we eat the body of Jesus and drink his blood by eating some bread and drinking some wine. This is not how we usually speak. This is not how things are or what can normally happen in human experience.

While it is easy to dismiss it all as incoherent nonsense, the paradoxical language tells us that we experience something supernatural when we participate in the Lord's Supper. The words and deeds of Jesus initiate us into a deep, unfathomable mystery that I want to unfold for you: the mystery of Christ's death on our behalf.

It is common to have meals at funerals to celebrate the lives and legacies of those who have died. Unlike these funeral meals, the Lord's Supper celebrates the sacrificial death of Jesus and the legacy that we receive from him by his death. By our participation in his body and blood we receive what he gained for us by his self-sacrifice, and proclaim the good news of his sacrificial death (1 Cor 10:16; 11:26).

It is surprising that in all his teaching Jesus did not explain the purpose of his death to his disciples before he died. He taught them repeatedly that he had to suffer, be rejected by his own people, be killed by them, and rise from the dead (Mark 8:31; 9:31; 10:32–34). Yet even though this was the goal of his mission as the Messiah, he was strangely reticent about what his death would accomplish, and how. Only once did he refer to his suffering and death as an act of redemption, an act by which he would give his life "as a ransom for many" (Mark 10:45).

In the Last Supper Jesus did not give any further direct explanation of what would be accomplished by his death. Instead of explaining the purpose of his suffering and death, he told his disciples to celebrate a strange meal in which he gave them his body to eat and his blood to drink. Through that meal he offered himself and the benefits of his death to them. That was why he longed so ardently to eat his last Passover with them (Luke 22:15). It announced what they would receive from him as their incarnate, crucified, and risen Lord. Through that sacred meal he showed them that his death was his bodily sacrifice for them and all people. His death was the perfect, definitive sacrifice for all the members of the human family. And the Lord's Supper is a perfect sacrificial banquet, similar to the holy meals that were a regular part of the divine service at the temple, and yet different from them.

In his last meal with his disciples Jesus claimed that the bread that he had blessed and broken and presented to his disciples was his body. The context of that claim helps clarify what it means. He had just shared the meat from the Passover lamb with them. Now he took some of the unleavened bread that was on the table, distributed it to them, and told them that it was his body, the body that replaced the Passover lamb in the new meal that he was providing for them.

T he Passover was originally celebrated by the families of the Israelites in Egypt, the land of slavery and death (Exod 12:1–13, 21–23). In it the blood from a young male lamb or goat was daubed on the doorframe of each of their houses so that God would "pass over" the door and spare their first-born sons from death (Exod 12:7, 13, 22–27). Then the roasted meat from it was eaten with unleavened bread by the family and its guests. In connection with that unique meal, which was observed in this way only once in Egypt, God also decreed that when they had entered the Promised Land, the Feast of the Passover should be celebrated each year on the same day and same month as a pilgrim festival (Exod 12:14–20, 24–27). It was called a pilgrim festival because it involved a journey for the Israelites with their families from their homes to God's "house" for a communal meal there in his presence. After they had arrived in the land of Canaan, they were to eat the Passover meal on the evening before the first of the seven days of the Feast of Unleavened Bread (Exod 12:1–20; 13:3–10).

They began to do that after their entry in the land (Josh 5:10–12). It was then that its celebration was associated first with the tabernacle and then with the temple (Deut 16:1–8). It was then that the blood from the slaughtered lambs was splashed against the altar for the burnt offering. It thereby became a "sacrifice," the offering of an animal for a holy meal in God's presence (Exod 12:27; Deut 16:2, 4–5). The holy meat from the lamb was eaten in a festive meal there in the vicinity of temple but not in its actual precincts. Thus Jesus and his disciples ate the Passover meal in the guest room of a house in Jerusalem (Luke 22:10–13).

The Passover feast of Jesus with his disciples in Jerusalem was a sacrificial meal. So too the Holy Supper that he established for them and for us. It is an even greater sacrificial meal, in which we do not eat the flesh of a dead animal but the living body of Jesus that is his sacrifice for us. He is therefore "our Passover lamb" who "has been sacrificed" for us (1 Cor 5:7). He is "the Lamb of God, who takes away the sin of the world" (John 1:29, 36). Thus when Jesus says that the bread is his body, he is speaking about his imminent self-sacrifice. Even so, he rather oddly shifts the focus to his body rather than on himself. He explains that further by adding that his body is for them, or, more precisely on their behalf (1 Cor 11:24); it is given on behalf of them (Luke 22:19).

Jesus's claim that his body is "given" is meant in two ways. The body that is given "for" them is also given "to" them to eat. The body which is given as a sacrifice on their behalf[14] is also offered as his gift to them. By his use of the timeless present participle "given" Jesus implies that the body which is about to be sacrificed on the cross will continue to be given to them in the future whenever they celebrate the meal. So what from the outside is an act of brutal violence is also, by God's design, an act of self-sacrificial love. The betrayal of Jesus by Judas who delivered him up into the hands of evil men (Matt 17:22; 26:2; Luke 24:7), was also a divine act by which he was "given up" to death for the trespasses of sinners by his heavenly Father (Rom 4:25; 8:32). In it he also "gave himself up" as a sacrifice on their behalf (Gal 2:20; Eph 5:2, 25).[15]

That sacrificial understanding of the Lord's Supper is confirmed by the reference to the bread and wine as the body and blood of Jesus. That is how the two separate parts of the sacrificed animals were described in Exodus 12:7–8 and Deuteronomy 12:27. The blood from all the animals was not eaten, but was offered to God on the altar to atone for the sins of his people. While the whole body of an animal presented as a burnt offering was burnt up on the altar, only some parts of the animals presented as peace offerings were burnt up (Lev 3:3–5, 9–11, 14–17). The rest of their meat was eaten in a holy meal (Lev 7:14–16). So in contrast with the normal procedure, Jesus does not just give only his body to eat, but also his blood to drink in his great sacrificial banquet.[16]

As a new Passover meal, the Lord's Supper was also the banquet of a new peace offering. It resembled and replaced the sacrificial banquets that the Israelites shared when they went up on pilgrimage to Jerusalem for the three great annual festivals—the Passover, Pentecost, and Booths. On these occasions they presented the so-called "peace offerings" (Lev 3; 7:11–16), in which the animals sacrificed also provided meat for a holy meal, a fellowship meal for purified people who were at peace with God and each other. These animals were offered from their flocks or herds as a "sacrifice of a peace offering" (Lev 3:1, 3, 6, 9). While the blood of the animals was splashed against the altar, the fat was burned on the altar to consecrate the meat (Lev 3:3–5, 9–11, 14–17). The rest of the sacrificed animal provided ample meat for the festive banquet, meat that was eaten by the Israelite households and their guests on the day it was offered or the next day (Lev 7:1–18), holy meat that God provided for his guests at the temple (Lev 19:5–8).

A special kind of peace offering was called a "sacrifice of praise," or "thanksgiving sacrifice," because it was offered as an act of thanksgiving to God for his generosity (Lev 7:12–15). It differed from a normal peace offering in two ways. On one hand, loaves of leavened and unleavened bread were offered with it. On the other hand, since it was presented as an act of praise to God for his goodness and thanksgiving for his bountiful blessings, the meal was most likely accompanied by a psalm of thanksgiving, such as Psalm 116.

Since most of us can eat meat every day if we wish, we do not appreciate what it meant for the Israelites, who seldom ate meat unless they were well-to-do, or were priests on duty at the temple. The only time all of them ate meat together was at these festive banquets. On these occasions God treated them as his honored, royal guests by giving them the best meat as their main course. No wonder these meals were times of great rejoicing (Deut 12:7, 12; 14:26)!

The Lord's Supper is not in itself a sacrifice in the strict sense of the word. It is a sacrificial banquet in which we receive Christ's sacrificed body and blood with thanksgiving and rejoicing. It is a Eucharist: an offering of thanksgiving and praise for Christ's sacrificial death.

In 1 Corinthians 10:14–22, Paul regards the Lord's Supper as a sacrificial banquet. On one hand, he contrasts it with the religious meals that were eaten by pagan people at the temples of their gods. The food that had been offered to the idols did not, as they fancied, establish communion with their gods, but instead associated them with the demons that were evoked by their offerings to these idols. On the other hand, Paul compares the Lord's Supper with the meals that Israelites ate as God's guests at the temple in Jerusalem. When the Israelites presented their peace offerings there, God provided them with holy meat to eat from his table, the altar for burnt offering. Through the holy meat that had been sanctified by its contact with the altar, they enjoyed fellowship with God and each other.

Paul therefore connects the Lord's Supper with these sacred meals, in which the Israelites ate the meat and bread from their peace offerings. He asks the congregation in Corinth, "The bread that we break, is it not a participation in the body of Christ?" (1 Cor 10:16). The bread that was broken and distributed was, in some supernatural way, the body of Jesus. So as they all shared in a piece of bread from a common loaf, they all shared in his body. As they ate that visible bread they also ate his invisible body together with it. Like the Israelites, the members of the church were guests at the Lord's table (1 Cor 10:21). Through their common participation in the holy body of Christ they had communion with God and each other.

Jesus instituted his Holy Supper as the great sacrificial banquet for all his disciples. In it he is both the host and the food. As their host he breaks the bread and feeds them with his holy body. It is his meal, his banquet. There they eat at his table. But he himself is also the food that they eat. His flesh is the bread that he gives for the life of the world (John 6:51). Just as all the Israelites who brought their peace offerings to the altar were guests at the Lord's table, so all Christians who eat his body in the Lord's Supper receive it from a new altar (Heb 13:10). They are united in holy communion with him and each other by eating this common food.

I n the Lord's Supper the risen Lord Jesus gives himself bodily to us, his guests. He who gave himself completely in his death on our behalf now gives himself to us with his crucified, risen body. In this meal he engages bodily with us in our whole humanity, and unites himself bodily with us, like a bridegroom with his bride, so that we in turn can offer ourselves with our bodies in service to him and in service to the people around us (Rom 12:1). That is the purpose of his death on our behalf. It is his heart's desire for us.

> Draw near and take the body of the Lord,
> And drink the holy blood for you outpoured;
> Offered was He for greatest and for least,
> Himself the victim and Himself the priest.

> "Draw Near and Take the Body of the Lord," verse 1
> Latin, 7th century[17]

VI

THE BLOOD OF THE COVENANT

Drink of it, all of you, for this is my blood of the covenant,
which is poured out for many for the forgiveness of sins.
Matthew 26:27–28 ESV

We are both fascinated and horrified by blood. Blood is a wonderful, powerful liquid that nourishes our bodies and keeps them alive. It carries oxygen and nutrients to our cells, and removes the wastes and toxins from our bodies. It protects us from infection by its antibodies and fights disease.

And so we value blood highly. Yet we are also rather squeamish about blood. We avoid contact with it, because we feel that it somehow stains us and makes us unclean. We even use *bloody* as a swear word, as if blood made things repulsive and disgusting.

It is no wonder, then, that many of us are put off by the whole business of sacrifices in the Old Testament, and the message of Christ's bloody death on the cross. If we are honest, we find the talk in the New Testament about the power of Christ's blood rather distasteful. Most of all, we're appalled at the thought of drinking blood. And so we avoid thinking and speaking about that much-neglected part of the Lord's Supper.

We aren't the only people who find that part of the Lord's Supper offensive. John tells us that many Jews who had been disciples of Jesus were so disgusted at his insistence that they drink his blood that they left him for good (John 6:60–66). And that was quite understandable, given their religious upbringing. Even though blood played an important part in the worship of God at the temple in Jerusalem, God had strictly forbidden the drinking of blood from any animal. So strict was this prohibition that they had to slaughter the animals in such a way that all the blood was drained from them, and poured out on the altar to atone for their sins (Lev 17:11). The life of the animal lay in its blood. Only godless pagans drank the blood of sacrificed animals to get vitality, energy, and power from it. The Israelites were not allowed to do that, or even to eat meat with blood in it. They could not get life-power for themselves from the blood, because all life belonged to God and God alone. In fact, God said that he would excommunicate anyone who drank the blood of any animal (Lev 17:13–14).

So you can well imagine how shocked the disciples were at the Last Supper when Jesus told them to drink his blood. He asked them to do something that, as Jews, they had never done before. They had to violate an ancient religious taboo that went back to God's covenant with Noah (Gen 9:4). Yet at the same time they would have sensed that Jesus was offering them something new. He linked his blood with the new covenant, his lasting legacy to them. By giving them his blood, he offered them something never given to his people before. Somehow he shared himself and his life with them in this strange, surprising way.

A t his Last Supper Jesus took a bowl of wine, gave thanks for it, and handed it to his disciples, so that they each in turn drank from this common cup. That in itself was unusual, because the normal custom was for the guests to pour some of the wine from the bowl into their own cups.

As he did this Jesus said three amazing things about the wine in that bowl. The wine was his blood, just as the bread he had given them was his body. It did not just resemble his blood or represent it; it was his blood. His blood was in the cup and given with the wine. That was rather odd, because Jesus had not yet died. He was still alive and visibly present with them. So as a living man he offered them his living, human blood to drink. It was something like a direct transfusion of blood into the veins of another person who needed it to survive.

Just as the blood from the animals slaughtered as sin offerings was caught in a bowl and "poured out" at the base of the altar at the temple (Lev 4:7, 18, 25, 30, 34; 8:15; 9:9), so the blood of Jesus was "poured out" as an offering for sin by his death on the cross. Now it was "poured out for many" to drink (Matt 26:28; Mark 14:24; Luke 22:20). Here Jesus echoes the prophecies in Isaiah that God's suffering servant would "sprinkle *many* nations" and "justify *many*," because he would bear "the sin of *many*" (Isa 52:15; 53:11–12). Jesus uses this adjective inclusively (in the Hebrew style) to refer to the whole of humanity rather than only a few people, such as his disciples or the Jews. So the same blood that Jesus would offer as a sacrifice for all people by his death on the cross was poured out in his Holy Supper for his twelve apostles and all his disciples to drink. Through the blood he poured out to atone for their sin he offered them "the forgiveness of sins" (Matt 26:28).

Jesus also called the wine "my blood of the covenant" (Matt 26:28; Mark 14:24). The wine was "the new covenant" in his blood (Luke 22:20; 1 Cor 11:25). He said this in the context of his imminent death. As the author of Hebrews notes, his covenant was his last will and testament for them as his chosen heirs (Heb 9:15–20). The Lord's Supper was not part of a bilateral agreement between Jesus and his disciples. It was gift of grace, a gratuitous endowment, something that was freely given as a favor on his part and freely received by faith in his promises. Thus the translators of the King James Version of the English Bible quite consistently referred to "the blood of the testament" rather than "the blood of the covenant,"[18] since it was by means of his blood that Jesus conferred to his disciples all that he had gained by his human life as God's Son and all that he would gain for them by his impending death. He not only ratified his testament for them with his blood, he also conferred their eternal inheritance on them through his blood. It was the means by which it was made available to them. By giving them his blood to drink, he shared the forgiveness of sins with them, along with all the other blessings he had gained from his heavenly Father for them.

Jesus's words about his covenant with his disciples recall two passages in the Old Testament. First, his mention of a new covenant alludes to God's promise in Jeremiah 31:31–34:

> Behold, the days are coming, declares the Lord, when I will make a new covenant with the house of Israel and the house of Judah, not like the covenant that I made with their fathers on the day when I took them by the hand to bring them out of the land of Egypt, my covenant that they broke, though I was their husband, declares the Lord. For this is the covenant that I will make with the house of Israel after those days, declares the Lord: I will put my law within them, and I will write it on their hearts. And I will be their God, and they shall be my people. And no longer shall each one teach his neighbor and each his brother, saying, "Know the Lord," for they shall all know me, from the least of them to the greatest, declares the Lord. For I will forgive their iniquity, and I will remember their sin no more.

By his institution of the Lord's Supper, Jesus fulfills this prophecy. The Israelites had broken the old covenant that God made with them after he freed them from oppression and the threat of extermination in Egypt and brought them into the Promised Land. Now, as a result of their apostasy, God was about to send them into exile in Babylon. But before that happened God gave them the promise of a new covenant in the future age of salvation, one that would replace the old covenant they had failed to keep. Like the old covenant, the new covenant also had to do with God's gift of his presence with them. Like the old covenant, the new covenant had to do with God's commitment to be their God and their calling to be his people—a calling they had failed to fulfill.

So God promised to make a new covenant with them that would differ from the old covenant in two ways. On one hand, God would teach them to serve him faithfully by writing his instruction in the hearts of all his people rather than on two tablets of stone. They would therefore all have equal access to God, and receive instruction from him through his word in their hearts. On the other hand, their access to God's grace would not depend on their observance of his law but on his forgiveness of their iniquity, his purification of their hearts, and the gift of a good conscience. God himself would cleanse them so thoroughly from their iniquity that he would no longer have any reason to remember it. They would be blameless in his sight. That divine pardon, that divine cleansing, is what Jesus gained for all people by his death, and gives to his disciples by his new covenant with them.

S econd, in his institution of the Lord's Supper Jesus also recalls the story of God's inauguration of his old covenant in Exodus 24:1–11. The Israelites were already God's people through God's covenant with Abraham and his descendants. At Mount Sinai Moses was the mediator of the covenant by which God made them "a holy nation," a covenant in which he appointed them to serve him as his royal priesthood by their participation in the divine service (Exod 19:6). There Moses consecrated them as a holy, priestly nation with blood of the covenant. After he had built an altar at the foot of the mountain, he commissioned some young men to offer burnt offerings and peace offerings to the Lord on it. But on this occasion the normal sequence of events was reversed. The blood from these offerings was not splashed against the altar before the offerings had been set on the altar, as usual, but after. Moses also disposed of the blood in a unique way. He put the blood into two separate basins. He took the first basin with one half of the blood and "threw" it on the altar to consecrate it. Then, after reading God's law to the people and hearing their agreement to obey it, he "threw" the other half of the blood on them, saying that it was the blood of God's covenant with them (Exod 24:8).

By means of that blood God not only made a bilateral covenant with them to be their God, but also consecrated them as his holy people. He consecrated them for their priestly service to him in their worship and life. After the consecration, their leaders who represented them had safe access to God's presence as his guests in a holy meal with him—a meal on Mount Sinai itself, rather than at its foot. There heaven came down to earth for them, shown by the sapphire pavement under God's feet; there they saw him as they ate and drank in his presence (Exod 24: 9–11).

The consecration of the Israelites with blood at Mount Sinai foreshadowed the subsequent consecration of Aaron and his sons as priests for service at the tabernacle. This was legislated by God in Exodus 29 and performed by Moses in Leviticus 8. In that ritual enactment blood played an important part. Moses smeared some of the blood from the ram for ordination on the right ear, the thumb of the right hand and the big toe of the priests to prepare them to hear God's holy word, handle his holy things, and stand in his holy sanctuary (Exod 29:19–20; Lev 8:23–24). Moses also took some of the holy blood from the altar, mixed it with the most holy anointing oil and "sprinkled" it on them and their vestments (Exod 29:21; Lev 8:30). The blood that was sprinkled on their bodies made and kept them holy.

In Exodus 24:8 Moses made this declaration as he sprinkled the blood of God's covenant on the Israelites at Mount Sinai: "This is the blood of the covenant that the Lord has made with you in accordance with all these words" (Exod 24:8 NIV). When Jesus instituted Holy Communion he recalled these words of Moses and reapplied them to it. In his celebration of the Passover meal with his disciples he established a new covenant with them as his last will and testament for them (Matt 26:28; Mark 14:24; Luke 22:20; 1 Cor 11:25), the new covenant by which they received their promised inheritance from Jesus (Matt 26:28; Heb 8:6–9:15). In it Jesus connected his sacrificial death to atone for the sins of all people on Good

Friday with the distribution of its benefits to God's people at all times and in all places after his resurrection. He did this by means of his blood. By their participation in the Lord's Supper they would receive the same blood to drink that he had poured out for them by his death on the cross. Thus Paul speaks about what Jesus does "now" with his blood (Rom 5:9; Eph 2:13). Jesus established the new covenant "by means of his blood" on the night before his crucifixion (Luke 22:20; 1 Cor 11:25) so that he could thereafter provide its blessings to all believers "by means of his blood" (Rom 3:25; 5:9; Eph 2:13; Heb 10:19; 13:20; Rev 1:5; 5:9; 7:14). They received these blessings from him "through his blood" (Acts 20:28; Eph 1:7; Heb 13:12; Rev 12:11), the holy blood that he brought with him into the heavenly sanctuary at his ascension (Heb 9:11–12).

What do we gain from drinking the blood of the risen Lord Jesus in his Holy Supper? In the old covenant the bodies of God's people were splashed with blood to cleanse them from spiritual impurity and to consecrate them for service as his holy, priestly people (Exod 24:8; 19:4–6). As holy people they could approach the earthly sanctuary and participate in the divine service where he met with them to bless them (Exod 20:24; 29:42–43).

In the new covenant, Jesus our great high priest, who now serves on our behalf before God the Father in heaven, sprinkles us with his holy blood (1 Pet 1:2; Heb 10:22; 12:24). He sprinkles it on our hearts, rather than just our bodies, so that we can serve the living God with a clear conscience as holy priests together with him in the heavenly sanctuary (Heb 9:13–14). By his blood Jesus cleanses us from the guilt of sin and our pollution by it (1 John 1:7, 9). He cleanses our consciences from the stain of all impurity, so that we can participate in the heavenly service of worship with pure hearts, without desecrating God's holiness with our impurity. Through the blood of the eternal covenant God the Father equips us with everything good, so that we can be sure he is pleased with us in our service of him (Heb 13:20–21).

Having atoned for our sins with his blood, Jesus now offers us the benefits of that atonement (Rom 3:24). By his blood Jesus pardons our sins and releases us from their effect on us; he extricates us from our guilt and its power over us; he sets us free from the accusation and condemnation of the devil (Matt 26:28; Rev 12:10–11). He redeems us from our sins by forgiving us (Eph 1:7). By his blood he justifies us before God the Father (Rom 5:9); by his blood he sets us free from our sins and makes us members of God's royal priesthood who have access to his gracious presence (Rev 1:5–6); he reconciles us with God and gives us peace through his blood (Col 1:20).

By his blood we who were once far from God have now been brought near to him (Eph 2:13). Through his blood we now have access to God the Father in one Spirit (Eph 2:18). Just as the high priest was able to enter the holy of holies on the Day of Atonement by means of the blood from the sin offerings (Lev 16:14–15), so we have the right to enter the heavenly sanctuary and approach God the Father there by the blood of

Jesus (Heb 10:19–22). It qualifies us for entry into God's heavenly presence with bold confidence in him and the complete assurance that he will welcome us and bless us.

By his blood Jesus sanctifies us inwardly and completely (Heb 10:29; 13:12). By ourselves we are not holy. But we are holy in him. He shares his own holiness with us, so that we are now as holy as he is. We are saints, holy people who stand before God together with his holy angels. Through the Holy Spirit Jesus sanctifies us by sprinkling us with his blood (1 Pet 1:2). We therefore depend on it for our sanctification. Like the priests in the Old Testament (Exod 29:21; Lev 8:30), our "robes" are made holy by the blood of the Lamb, so that we can stand with Jesus in the presence of his heavenly Father (Rev 7:14).

All that and much more is ours by faith in Jesus and his blood—the blood we receive from him in Holy Communion. Through his blood we are blood brothers and blood sisters with him. As coheirs with him we have a foretaste of our heavenly inheritance already in this life here on earth.

Fountain of goodness, Jesus, Lord and God:
Cleanse us, unclean, with Thy most cleansing blood;
Increase our faith and love, that we may know
The hope and peace which from Thy presence flow.

"Thee We Adore, O Hidden Savior," verse 4
Thomas Aquinas[19]

GRANT US, THEREFORE,
GRACIOUS LORD,
SO TO EAT THE FLESH
OF YOUR DEAR SON
JESUS CHRIST,
AND TO DRINK HIS BLOOD

VII

THE UNSEEN HOST

Then they told what had happened on the road and how he
had been made known to them in the breaking of the bread.
Luke 24:35 NRSV

e might assume that the meals Jesus shared with people throughout his ministry culminate in the Last Supper. But Luke tells us this is not so. According to his report, they reach their goal in the journey of Jesus with two disciples on Easter Sunday, and his supper with them in Emmaus that evening (Luke 24:13–35). For Luke, this was the last of seven meals in which Jesus was present with people as either a guest or a host. In fact on that occasion he was with them as both their guest and their host. This story shows us why Jesus participated in the first six meals, and how all of them throw light on the ongoing celebration of the Lord's Supper by his disciples after his death and resurrection.

The first meal is the great banquet that Levi hosted in Jesus's honor (Luke 5:27–32) after Jesus called him. It was the kind of lavish reception that was offered for a very important person in the ancient world. Besides Jesus, his disciples and Levi's colleagues were there as his guests. What a mixed company! Because Levi (who was also called Matthew) was a tax collector for the Roman government, he was a social and religious outcast. According to the strict interpretation of God's law espoused by the scribes who were experts in its application and the Pharisees who were ardent in its observance, Levi was a "sinner," an unclean person who had broken God's law so blatantly that God had rejected him. They also held that anyone who joined in a meal with tax collectors would be infected by them and become spiritually unclean like them. Levi was therefore excluded from the temple and its holy meals. No wonder then that critics of Jesus were horrified that he ate and drank with sinners such as Levi. They held that he desecrated his holiness by his association with them. Jesus, surprisingly, does not dispute their judgment. Instead of that, he compares his behavior to that of a compassionate physician who risks severe infection by sick people in order to heal them. He also compares his self-righteous critics with healthy people have no need of him and his help. Jesus consorts with sinners and calls them to repentance so they can receive forgiveness and be restored to spiritual health. By his presence at his meals with them he offers them divine healing by their repentance and reception of divine pardon.

In the second meal Luke reports, Jesus is the guest of a Pharisee called Simon (Luke 7:36–50). On this occasion a woman who was a notorious "sinner" intruded in the guise of a lowly servant to "wash" his feet with her tears, wipe them dry with her hair, kiss them with her lips, and anoint them with a lavish amount of perfume. Even though Simon said nothing, he was silently appalled by her rash behaviour and the compliance of Jesus with it. Jesus must have known that she was desecrating his holiness by her impurity. If Jesus was a prophet, he should have recognized her spiritual state and refused to let her treat him like this. But as a prophet who knew what Simon was thinking and why the woman was washing and anointing his feet, Jesus explained her unusual behaviour as gesture of grateful devotion and love for the forgiveness she had received from him. He therefore reassured her that she was indeed forgiven.[20] Since she had been forgiven, she was not at all out of place at the table with Jesus. Since she had been freed from the guilt and power of sin by her faith in Jesus, she could go from that place in peace, with a good conscience, and without fear of condemnation by God. Jesus was teaching Simon a lesson in divine mercy and love.

In the third meal, Jesus feeds five thousand disciples with five loaves and two fish in Bethsaida, at the end of a day in which he had taught them about God's kingdom and healed those who were sick (Luke 9:10–17). On this occasion he was the host of the meal. Then, as he later did at the Last Supper, he blessed the food, broke the bread, and gave it to his disciples to distribute to the hungry crowd. Amazingly, they had so much bread that that there were twelve baskets of leftover pieces. By his depiction of Jesus as the host of those he had taught, Luke shows us that this miraculous meal foreshadows the far greater meal in which he would provide his body with some bread for an unlimited number of guests, bread that satisfies their spiritual hunger and sustains their souls with heavenly food.

In the fourth meal, Jesus is a guest of a leading Pharisee in a holy banquet on a Sabbath day, when all work was strictly forbidden (Luke 14:1–24). On that occasion an uninvited man with dropsy from the accumulated fluid in his body appeared before Jesus. Since his swollen skin made him ritually unclean, he was disqualified from participation in the services of worship at the temple and the synagogue (Lev 13:2, 10). The host of the meal and his religious guests watched Jesus critically to see whether he would pollute himself by touching the unclean man, or break the Sabbath by healing him. But that did not hamper Jesus at all. He reached out to the man and healed him. He removed the man's impurity and shared his own health with him. When he had healed the man, Jesus challenged his critics by contrasting their criticism of the "work" that he had done on the Sabbath with their self-serving application of God's law. While they forbade his "work" of healing a man whose life was threatened by dropsy, they held that they were allowed to save the life of their own son or ox that had fallen in a well on the Sabbath by rescuing them from drowning. Why should the healing of that man be forbidden if the rescue of a son or ox from drowning was permitted? Then Jesus called them to repentance by telling them to take the lowliest seats of honor at the table for the banquet (14:7–11), by urging them to show hospitality to those who could not repay them rather than to their friends and brothers, their relatives and rich neighbours (14:12–14), and by warning them that their seats at the heavenly banquet would be given to others if they rejected God's invitation to his royal banquet (14:15–24).

Jesus was the guest of another tax collector, named Zacchaeus, in Luke 19:1–10. On this occasion Jesus did not wait for an invitation from Zacchaeus but told him that he had to stay at his house that very day. Once again some bystanders were critical of Jesus for choosing to be the guest of a sinner. Jesus did not argue with them, but announced that by his visit he was bringing salvation to Zacchaeus's house—and not just to him, but to all the lost people he had come to seek and save. Indeed that was his mission as God's representative: to seek and save the lost. That's why Jesus invited himself to be the guest of this sinner. He associated with sinners in order to take their sin on himself and save them from it by his sacrificial death.[21]

The sixth meal is the holy Passover banquet of Jesus with his twelve apostles in Luke 22:14–38. In it Jesus was the host of a new meal that surpassed all the previous meals. In it he gave them his own body to eat with the bread and his own blood to drink with the wine. In it Jesus the host also honored his apostles by waiting on them and declaring, "I am among you as the one who serves" (Luke 22:27). His use of the present tense implies that he would continue to be with them as their waiter in every future celebration of his Holy Supper. He also appointed them to cohost it with him, and gave them an example of how they should exercise that role as his royal agents by serving their own guests (Luke 22:25–30).

T he last, conclusive meal of Jesus occurred on the evening of Easter Sunday (Luke 24:13–35) and involved two disciples of Jesus, one of whom was Cleopas (24:18), who may have been the uncle of Jesus (John 19:25). These disciples had heard the weird report of some women in their company who had gone to the tomb of Jesus to look for his body. They had seen some angels who told them that Jesus was alive. Some other members of their group confirmed what the women had said, but these two disciples did not yet believe that Jesus was alive. They were so appalled at his crucifixion that they could not fathom why he had to suffer and die to redeem Israel.

When Jesus joined them on their journey and engaged them in a conversation about their disappointment at his apparent failure, they did not at first recognize him. As far as they knew he was dead and gone. So Jesus made himself known to them in two stages and in two locations. First, he preached himself to them from the Old Testament as he walked with them. Yet even though their hearts burned with joy as he spoke, they still did not recognize him. Then, when they urged him to stay overnight with them as their guest, he acted as if he was their host when they sat down for the evening meal. He took the bread, gave thanks, broke it, and gave it to them, just as he had done when he instituted his Holy Supper three nights earlier, and before that when he had fed five thousand people at Bethsaida. Then their eyes were opened and they recognized him "in the breaking of the bread" (24:35). That is Luke's name for the Lord's Supper in the book of Acts (2:42, 46; 20:7). As soon as they recognized him, he vanished from their sight. When they saw him they did not recognize him; when they recognized him they no longer saw him.

By giving us such a detailed account of this event, Luke shows us how all the other meals culminated in the regular celebration of the Lord's Supper by his disciples. Like some of them it is a meal in which he nourishes them in a miraculous way. Like others it is a meal in which he calls sinners to repentance and heals them. It is also a meal in which he offers forgiveness to sinners, restoration to lost souls, and salvation from condemnation. Like all of them it is a joyful meal in which prodigal children are welcomed home by their heavenly Father, and their grumpy siblings are urged to celebrate their homecoming (Luke 15:22–24, 32).

In each of these meals Jesus teaches his guests about himself and what he gives them as the Messiah. They are meals that teach. So in keeping with that purpose, Luke uses the seventh meal in his Gospel to tell the disciples of Jesus what he does for them and gives to them when they gather to celebrate the Lord's Supper each Sunday. There the risen Lord Jesus meets with them as their invisible host and unseen guest. There he discloses himself to them as he feeds them with his sacrificed body and blood. There he gives himself bodily to them. There they listen to him and recognize him and his gracious presence by faith, as he travels with them on their journey through life on earth.

TABLE 3: THE MEALS OF JESUS IN LUKE'S GOSPEL

CITATION	LOCATION	STATUS OF JESUS
Luke 5:27–39	Matthew's home	Invited guest
Luke 7:36–50	Simon the Pharisee's home	Invited guest
Luke 9:10–17	The town of Bethsaida	Host
Luke 14:1–24	A ruler of the Pharisee's home for a Sabbath meal	Guest
Luke 19:1–10	Zacchaeus's home in Jericho	Self-invited guest
Luke 22:7–34	The upper guest room of a house in Jerusalem	Host and waiter
Luke 24:13–35	With two disciples in Emmaus	Guest and host

NATURE OF THE HOST	THE GIFTS OF JESUS
Tax collector and sinner	Call to repentance and reception of forgiveness
Self-righteous Pharisee	Forgiveness of sins
Jesus the Messiah	Supernatural nourishment
Critical leader of the Pharisees	Life-saving healing for an unclean man
Tax collector and sinner	Salvation for lost people
Self-sacrificial Messiah	His sacrificed body and blood
Risen Messiah	Self-proclamation and self-disclosure

All these meals that Luke records in his Gospel need to be taken together. They throw light on each other and the involvement of Jesus in them as either a guest or a host. They culminate in the appearance of the risen Lord Jesus to two of his disciples at Emmaus on the eve of his resurrection. In that meal he is present with them as both their guest and their host. Through the record of these meals Luke proclaims and explains the nature and purpose of the Lord's Supper to us, as summarised in table 3.

What then do these stories tell us the risen Lord Jesus provides for his guests in the meal that he hosts for them, the meal in which he serves them and discloses himself to them? He provides supernatural, life-sustaining nourishment for them as his disciples and satisfies them with the abundant food (Luke 9:10–17). Like a good physician, he calls sinners who are spiritually sick with a terminal sickness to come to him so that he can heal them (Luke 5:31–32). He heals those who are physically sick, like the unclean man with dropsy (Luke 14:1–6). He welcomes the worst of sinners who reach out to him in faith and uses his divine authority to pardon them, assure them of God's acceptance of them, and give them the peace that only God can provide (Luke 7:47–50). Last and best of all, he seeks and saves the people who are lost and lonely because they are far from God and cannot save themselves from condemnation to eternal death and destruction by their moral rectitude and religiosity (Luke 19:1–10). He justifies those who cannot justify themselves. In his Supper he gives himself to them and takes them as they are. By his hospitality he takes on their sickness and gives them his health. He takes on their uncleanness and gives them his purity. He takes on their sin and gives them his righteousness. He takes on their guilt and gives them his innocence. He takes on their shame and shares his honor with them. Their place at his table on earth anticipates and discloses their place honor with his royal Father in the heavenly feast (Luke 14:7–24).

In the state where I live there is a small country church that I love. It is not far from where I was born, and where I lived for the first fifteen years of my life. It is a simple old building that is quite ordinary apart from its ornate wooden altar. On the altar are the words, "For Sinners Only!"

I love that church because it reminds me that the Lord's Supper is a meal in which the risen Lord Jesus meets with repentant sinners, like you and me and all his disciples. When I first visited it with my family, as a teenager with a bad conscience, I was struck by its message. It has stuck with me ever since, and I often remember it joyfully when I receive Holy Communion.

Come, risen Lord, and deign to be our guest;
No, let us be your guests and with you dine;
At your own table now be manifest
In your own sacrament of bread and wine.

We meet as in the upper room they met;
Now at the table, blessing, yet you stand:
"This is my body": this you give us yet;
Faith still receives the cup as from your hand.

One body we, one body who partake,
One church united in communion blessed;
One name we bear, one bread of life we break,
With all your saints on earth and saints at rest.

One with each other, Lord, and one in you,
Who are one Savior and one living head;
Open our eyes to see with vision true;
Be known to us in breaking of the bread.

"Come, Risen Lord and Deign to Be Our Guest,"
George Wallace Briggs[22]

VIII

SOUND REMEMBRANCE

This is my body, which is for you. Do this in remembrance of me.
... This cup is the new covenant in my blood. Do this,
as often as you drink it, in remembrance of me.
1 Corinthians 11:24–25 ESV

We forget most of what has happened to us—which is just as well. Otherwise our minds would be overwhelmed with trivia and we would be unable to function properly. Yet even though we need to forget what is unimportant to us, our survival depends on our recollection of what is vital for us. Our memory of what is important governs how we live and determines whether we thrive.

This is most evident in people who suffer from dementia. Even though they remain conscious, they live fragmented lives, without a proper sense of their past, present, or future.

Everything is jumbled up for them. They have lost the plot of their life. Its details make little or no sense. They can no longer recall its whole story, but only unrelated episodes. Nor can they recall how other people are connected to them, even the members of their family. They no longer know what to expect, because they have forgotten who they are and what has happened to them. Even so, their bodies still seem to remember what their minds have forgotten.

Even if we have sound minds, we cannot always rely on our memory because our minds are so easily swayed by subjective influences and negative emotions. Memory is always fragile and often inaccurate. Unless it has fixed checkpoints and reliable external points of reference, it can be readily distorted by what we fancy and desire. It is obscured by guilt at the bad things we have done and erased by trauma from the bad things that have happened to us. Worst of all, memory is misconstrued by hostility and distorted by hatred. Its accuracy depends on its grounding in what has really been said and what has really happened.

Sound remembrance frees us from being imprisoned in the here and now. It not only locates us in particular places at particular times, but also shows us how to transcend them. It relates us to what has happened in our past and forecasts what is likely to happen in the future. My marriage is a good example of this. Even though I was married to my wife Claire fifty-six years ago, I am still married now and will be married until one of us dies. My remembrance of her and our life together grounds me. It tells me who I am—the same person I once was and still am and always will be, as long as I live.

This aspect of remembrance was recently brought home to me rather powerfully by my visit to the farm in the Barossa Valley in South Australia, where I spent the first fifteen years of my life, and the church that was the spiritual home of my family. That visit revived my memory of many things I had largely forgotten. It reminded me how what happened in my boyhood makes me the person that I now am. Because we visited the cemetery where some of my ancestors lie buried and where my wife and I have decided to be buried, I was also reminded of what lies ahead for me: my bodily death and the resurrection by which I will join those who have gone before me. I remembered that my whole life cycle is part of that larger story—an eternal story, the story of God's journey with all his people.

That pilgrimage helped me understand why Jesus, when he instituted his Holy Supper, said, "Do this in remembrance of me" (Luke 22:19; 1 Cor 11:24, 25). The Lord's Supper is a memorial meal. Since Jesus said this on the night before he died, we all too readily regard it as something like the annual commemoration of the death of our parents or others we love, or an occasional visit to their graves or the places where their ashes are interred. Even though we do remember the death of Jesus and our legacy from him in this memorial meal, it differs significantly from the usual commemoration of someone's death.

We usually think of the past when we speak about what we remember. That is also true, in part, for the Lord's Supper. When we celebrate it we remember the death of Jesus and its significance for us. We remember what happened to him long ago and what he accomplished for us by his death on the cross. Yet when Jesus told the apostles to host his Supper in remembrance of him, he also wanted them to remember his ongoing presence with them (Luke 22:27).

We do not remember him the same way I remembered my dead ancestors when I visited the cemetery where they lie buried. Just as Paul urged Timothy to "remember Jesus Christ, risen from the dead" (2 Tim 2:8), we remember him as our living Lord, who died but is now alive. We remember and recognize him as our unseen host, just as the two disciples did at Emmaus (Luke 24:30–31). We remember that he travels with us in our journey through life, and we remember what he gives us as our divine and human host. At the same time, we also recall what he has promised to do for us through our union with him and our reception of his body and blood. We remember what he has done, is doing, and will yet do for us.

We may also distinguish between the Lord's Supper as a memorial meal of Jesus and our communal remembrance of him as we participate in it, just as we may distinguish between a birthday meal for a person and the memories it evokes. Jesus established it to remind us of his death and how we now benefit from it. But he also established it to get us to remember him physically by what we eat and drink, do and say, and mentally by what we think and feel, imagine and desire. Since it presents us with what we need to remember about Jesus, it shapes what we remember and how. It grounds our memory of him and keeps it fixed on a strong foundation.

T he Lord's Supper is a memorial meal. In it Jesus reminds us of his death both by what he does and by what he says. These two things belong together. Jesus reminds us of his death by taking bread and a cup of wine, giving thanks, and giving the bread and wine to us to eat and drink. Yet by themselves these three acts merely disclose that he is the host of the meal—and little more than that! They do not show us that this meal is a memorial banquet, or how. But the words of Jesus make it a memorial of his death. They tell us what Jesus has done for us by his death and what we receive from him because of it. They tell us that Jesus remembers us by hosting this meal and reminds us of his presence with us there.

When Paul repeats the command of Jesus to celebrate this meal in remembrance of him (1 Cor 11:23–25), he tells us that Jesus teaches us two things about his death in it. On one hand Jesus says, "This is my body, which is for you."[23] So the bread is his body, the body that Jesus gave as a vicarious sacrifice for us and all his disciples. The same body that Jesus sacrificed for us is given to us in the Lord's Supper. It is therefore a memorial of his sacrificial death, the death that he suffered on our behalf, his life-giving death that has freed us from eternal death. In this memorial meal he gives us his bodily life at the cost of his bodily death.

On the other hand, Jesus says, "This cup is the new covenant in my blood." The wine is his blood and the new covenant that is given in it. The blood is the new covenant, the New Testament, by which Jesus commits himself to us and gives us all that he has gained for us by his life in the body and his bodily death for us. It is the blood by which we are cleansed from sin and made holy. As we drink it we inherit what Jesus has won for us by his death on our behalf. It provides us with a foretaste of our heavenly inheritance.

The most remarkable thing about this memorial meal is its emphasis on what Jesus now gives to his disciples in it as a result of his sacrificial death for them. He gives them his body to eat and his blood to drink. He gives himself with his body to them to make them one body with him and each other (1 Cor 10:16–17). He gives them his blood as his new covenant with them by which he conveys what he has, his heritage, as a gift to them. As children of God and coheirs with Jesus they receive the spiritual blessings that Jesus has as God's Son. The gift of his body and blood is meant to bring Jesus to remembrance for them.

We remember the people we know by greeting them personally by name when we meet them and engaging in conversation with them. We remember what they have done for us and given us by thanking them. We remember what they are like by telling others about their association with us and how well they have treated us. How then do we remember Jesus in the

Lord's Supper? Even though Jesus tells us that this holy meal is meant to awaken and confirm our remembrance of him, he does not tell us how we are to remember him. Nor does Luke tell us what we are to do to remember him when he reports the instruction of Jesus to his apostles to celebrate that meal in remembrance of him (Luke 22:19).

But in 1 Corinthians 11:26, Paul does. There he gives us this rather general, helpful explanation: "For as often as you eat this bread and drink the cup, you proclaim the Lord's death until he comes." Our remembrance of Jesus is a communal, physical, and verbal recollection of his death.

E ven though the Lord's Supper engages each of us personally, it also evokes and confirms our communal remembrance of Jesus, our common memory of him. Despite all our personal differences, we all share a common meal; we all eat the same bread, which is his body, and drink from the same cup of wine, which is his blood. Our common reception of his body makes us one body with Jesus and each other (1 Cor 10:16–17). Our common experience of this meal affirms and confirms our common memory of his death and its significance for us. We who are one body therefore have one mind. We share the same confession of faith in Jesus. All this is of great value for us in Western societies such as the United States or Australia. It frees us from the ravages of individualism and the curse of loneliness for life in community.

Our communal remembrance is not only mental. It is also physical. We remember our Lord's death by eating the bread and drinking the wine. We remember him by what we do as a community, just as all those who participate in a birthday party for someone remember that person with a common meal and customary ritual observances. Our physical participation in the Lord's Supper is a communal commemoration, a common acknowledgment of him as our Lord, a common physical confession of faith in him.

There is still another even more important dimension to our physical and mental remembrance of Jesus. Paul says that when we eat and drink we "proclaim" the Lord's death. That verb indicates that those who participate in the Lord's Supper remember Jesus by what they all have to say in that meal. They remember him and his death by their spoken words, their communal proclamation.

This may refer to one or all the following three kinds of speech. It may refer to the recitation of the words of Jesus about his meal by the minister who presides at the meal together with Jesus. On behalf of Jesus and the congregation, his ministers remember him and his death by the recitation of his words to consecrate the bread and wine as the body and blood of Jesus, and when they distribute these gifts to their recipients. The recipients in turn remember Jesus by saying "Amen."

This proclamation may also refer to the recitation by the minister of a prayer of thanksgiving that includes the words of Jesus in the narrative of his institution of the Lord's Supper, the Lord's Prayer, and other prayers. The customary name for this is the Eucharistic Prayer. The congregation affirms it and owns it as its prayer with its Amen and other responses.

Most likely, it refers to the remembrance of Jesus and his death by the whole congregation in the wide range of spoken or sung prayers and praises that make up the traditional orders of service for the Lord's Supper from the early church to the present day. In them the congregation remembers the Lord Jesus and his death, whether by declaration or acclamation, thanksgiving or adoration, petitionary or intercessory prayer. Take the ancient song about Jesus as the Lamb of God, which is still sung in many Western churches before the reception of the Supper. In it the congregation recalls the declaration of John the Baptist in John 1:29 and acclaims Jesus as the Lamb who takes away the sin of the world before it pleads for his mercy and peace for itself and all people. This is consistent the teaching of remembrance in the Psalter and by Paul in his letters. There he reminds the congregations and the ministers he addresses that he remembers them regularly by thanking God for them and praying for them (Rom 1:8–10; Eph 1:1–22; Phil 1:3–6; Col 1:3–4; 1 Thess 1:2–3; 2 Tim 1:3; Phlm 4–5). We therefore remember Jesus and his death by receiving his body and blood with adoration and praise, thanksgiving and prayer.

O ur memories can be sound or unsound, wholesome or toxic, because our remembrance is governed by the state of our conscience. If we have a bad conscience that is tainted by the bad things we have done, our guilt has a negative impact on what we remember, and how it affects us. When we remember our misdeeds, we excuse ourselves and try to justify what we have done; we blame others and criticize them. Or else we accuse and condemn ourselves; we regard ourselves as worthless and punish ourselves to make up for what we have done. But if we have a good conscience that comes from forgiveness and acceptance, we are not obsessed by the remembrance of our wrongdoing or oppressed by its destructive effect on us. We remember that we are pardoned and loved.

That is what Jesus does for us in his Holy Supper. He replaces our guilt and shame with his justification and vindication. By cleansing our conscience and sharing his holiness with us he frees us from our toxic, destructive memories. We remember his goodness and mercy and love. We remember that we are justified by his grace through our trust in him. We remember that we have nothing to fear from God because he has saved us from condemnation and rejection.

> According to thy gracious word,
> In meek humility,
> This will I do, my dying Lord,
> I will remember thee.

Thy body, broken for my sake,
My bread from heaven shall be;
Thy testamental cup I take,
And thus remember thee.

When to the cross I turn my eyes,
And rest on Calvary,
O Lamb of God, my sacrifice,
I must remember thee:

And when these failing lips grow dumb,
And mind and memory flee,
When thou shalt in thy kingdom come,
Then, Lord, remember me.

"According to Thy Gracious Word," verses 1, 2, 4, and 6
James Montgomery[24]

THAT OUR SINFUL BODIES
MAY BE MADE CLEAN BY HIS BODY,
AND OUR SOULS WASHED
THROUGH HIS PRECIOUS BLOOD

IX

BREAD FROM HEAVEN

Jesus then said to them, "Truly, truly, I say to you, … my Father gives you the true bread from heaven. For the bread of God is he who comes down from heaven and gives life to the world."
John 6:33 ESV

We need good food to nourish us physically. Wholesome food keeps us alive and healthy with the nutrients it supplies. Unwholesome food impairs our health by polluting our bodies. That's why we are so concerned with what we eat. We know that a good life depends on a good diet.

But we don't always agree on what is the best diet for us. Does a diet of fresh fruit and vegetables keep us in good health with physical vitality and abundant energy? Does a low carbohydrate diet supplemented with the right kinds of protein reduce our weight and keep us fit? Does an organic diet prevent us from polluting our bodies with processed food and chemical additives? Does a liver-cleansing diet flush out the pollutants from our bodies? Does a vegetarian diet enhance our physical and mental well-being? Is there a diet that is good for our mental health? And so on.

It is true that we need to eat good food to nourish our bodies and keep them physically alive. But do we also need good food to sustain our spiritual health? If so, what kind of food? In John 6:25–59 Jesus teaches us that we do depend on one kind of food and drink for our spiritual vitality. It is the food and drink that he supplies in the meal that he hosts for us here on earth, a meal in which he provides us with "the bread of God," "the true bread from heaven" (John 6:32–33). That bread does not just sustain our spiritual life but actually gives us eternal life. It is, in fact, the only bread that gives us life.

T he occasion for this instruction was a miracle Jesus performed (John 6:1–15), the fourth of seven Messianic signs John records. These signs, which foreshadowed his death and resurrection, were meant to show his disciples that he was the Messiah, God's Son, and that they would receive life through their faith in him as their risen Lord (John 20:30–31).

That fourth miracle was his feeding of five thousand men with five barley loaves and two fish on a mountain by the Sea of Galilee. John's account of this event depicts Jesus as the host of that meal, who takes the loaves of bread and fish, gives thanks for them, and distributes them to the seated crowd. Jesus not only fed the crowd with the food he provided but also instructed his disciples to gather twelve baskets of leftover bread so that none of it would "perish" (John 6:12). Then when the people tried to make him their king, he withdrew from them and rejoined them the next day in the synagogue in Capernaum. There he taught them the purpose of that miracle in his discourse with them in John 6:25–59.

The texts for this sermon were the two readings from the Old Testament for that service in the synagogue: Exodus 16, with its story of God's gift of manna as food for the Israelites in the desert, and Psalm 78, with its warning to God's people about their failure to learn from God's gift of manna to trust in him (78:22–25). The sermon's theme was God's announcement in Exodus 16:4 that he would silence the grumbles of the Israelites about their lack of food in the desert by sending them bread from heaven. There he gave them a daily ration of bread, with a double amount on the sixth day to be eaten on the Sabbath. That ration of bread "perished" if it was kept any longer (Exod 16:19–21). God's daily provision of manna continued until his people entered into the Promised Land (Exod 16:34–35; Josh 5:10–12). This bread from heaven was his food for them on that journey. Both Jesus and his crowd of hearers took that story as a prophecy of what God would do for his people in the age to come through their coming King, the promised Messiah.

Jesus's sermon in John 6:25–58 was a dialogue between Jesus as the teacher and the congregation in Capernaum as his students, a discussion in which he dealt with their legitimate questions, their request for practical help, and the objections of some to what he was teaching. His audience in the synagogue was the crowd he had fed the previous day with the loaves and the fish (6:22–25). Jesus first answered their three questions—when he had come there from the other side of the lake where he had fed them (6:25), what they had to do to gain a lasting supply of food from him (6:28), and what further sign he would perform for them to believe in him (6:30-31). Then Jesus responded to their request to give them the bread of God (6:34). After his presentation of himself to them as the bread of life, Jesus addressed a part of the crowd that John called "the Jews,"[25] those who grumbled about his all-too-human origin and credentials (6:42) and argued with each other on how he could give them his flesh to eat (6:52).

In each case Jesus taught his hearers about himself as "the bread from heaven" as he led them ever deeper into what he had been commissioned to provide for them, and how. He began by contrasting the perishable food they sought from Jesus, the food their ancestors ate and died, with the imperishable food he would give them, "the food that endures to eternal life" (6:26–27). Then he asserted that all that they needed to do to gain that eternal food was to believe in him whom God had sent (6:29). He also declared that his Father would give them "the bread of

God" to eat, the true life-giving bread from heaven (6:32–33). In the last three parts of the discourse Jesus told them that he himself was "the bread of life." Thus those who came to him and believed in him would have eternal life even now, and he would raise them from the dead on the last day (6:38–40, see also 6:44, 47, 54). Then he added that since he was "the bread of life," "the living bread that came down from heaven," those who ate his flesh would "not die" but "live forever" (6:50–51). Then his sermon culminated in this startling conclusion:

> Truly, truly, I say to you, unless you eat the flesh of the Son of Man and drink his blood, you have no life in you.[26] Whoever feeds on my flesh and drinks my blood has eternal life, and I will raise him up on the last day. For my flesh is true food and my blood is true drink. Whoever feeds on my flesh and drinks my blood abides in me, and I in him. As the living Father sent me, and I live because of the Father, so whoever feeds on me, he also will live because of me. This is the bread that came down from heaven, not like the bread the fathers ate, and died. Whoever feeds on this bread will live forever. (John 6:53–58)

Jesus claimed to be himself the bread from heaven who would feed people on earth with his flesh and blood. He anticipated what he would do as the Son of Man and God's Son, who would give his flesh for the life of the world.

TABLE 4: THE STRUCTURE AND PURPOSE OF THE DISCOURSE OF JESUS WITH HIS AUDIENCE IN JOHN 6:25–58

	THE REMARKS OF THE CONGREGATION	THE TEACHING OF JESUS
6:25, 26–27	**Question 1, from the crowd:** "Rabbi, when did you come here?"	They should not seek perishable food but work for the eternal food given by the Son of Man whom God the Father has chosen.
6:28, 29–30	**Question 2, from the crowd:** "What must we do, to be doing the works of God?"	The work of God is faith in him whom God has sent.
6:30–31, 32–33	**Question 3, from the crowd:** "Then what sign do you do, that we may see and believe you?"	My Father gives you the true, life-giving bread from heaven.
6:34, 35–40	**Request by the crowd:** "Sir, give us this bread always."	Jesus is the bread of life, who gives eternal life to those who believe in him.
6:41–42, 43–51	**Question 4, from the grumbling Jews:** How does this son of Joseph now say, I have come down from heaven?	Jesus is the living bread who gives himself as food, so that those who believe in him will live forever.
6:52, 53–58	**Question 5 by the disputing Jews:** "How can this man give us his flesh to eat?"	Jesus gives himself with his flesh and blood as the bread of eternal life.

There is a sequence of disclosure in Jesus's teaching about the bread from heaven. He connects God's gift of manna to his people in the desert with his gift of the true bread from heaven, with himself as the bread of life, and then, finally and conclusively, with his flesh and blood as life-giving bread. This teaching of Jesus about the bread from heaven is summarized in his response to three questions addressed to him by his crowd of hearers that culminate in their request to him for the gift of heavenly bread. His answer to that request results in two questions his critics ask about him and his teaching.

In this discourse Jesus addresses our limited human capacity to understand heavenly things. He challenges us to join the crowd of disciples, listen to what he offers us as God's Son, and ask him for the bread from heaven. His words invite us to be humble receivers of the food he promises, rather than argumentative critics who reject him and what he offers. Like Nicodemus in John 3:9–15, we need to let him teach us heavenly things—things we cannot fathom unless he initiates us into the mystery of eternal life. He does not invite us to speculate about what he says, but to participate in the meal by tasting the food he provides. The proof of that food is in eating and drinking it.

I n this discourse Jesus first speaks to us in earthly terms about the food we eat, the food that sustains our human life on earth. Then he contrasts that earthly, life-sustaining food with God's heavenly, life-giving food, the food we receive from him; he contrasts our perishable food that cannot prevent us from dying with God's imperishable food that keeps us alive forever (John 6:50, 58). No earthly food can do that for us. By this comparison of what we know with what we don't know he teaches us that he was sent to earth to deliver eternal life to us and to show us how we can receive it from him.

This is how that happens. As God's eternal Son, Jesus shares in the eternal life of his heavenly Father. His living, life-giving Father has sent him to earth to share our human life in the flesh in order to share his divine life with us (John 6:57). We therefore receive eternal life from God the Father through faith in him. As the Son of Man, the human son and heir of Adam, he provides us with the food that gives eternal life (6:27). God the Father gives us Jesus as the true bread from heaven; he is the bread of God that comes down from heaven and gives life to us here on earth (6:33). The Father's purpose, his mission for Jesus, is for him to raise up people from the dead on the last day and to give eternal life to all who believe in him. In fact, when we look to him and believe in him, we receive eternal life from him already (6:38–40).

The Father himself teaches us this practically. Through his word he draws us to Jesus so that we receive eternal life from him (6:44–47). So Jesus is the bread of life who satisfies our human hunger and thirst for a life that never ends (6:35). Since he is "the living bread that came down from heaven," anyone who eats this bread will not die but will live forever (John 6:48–51).

Up to this point it's easy to fancy that Jesus is speaking metaphorically about himself as the bread from heaven, and about eating as a figure of speech for intellectual understanding. But in John 6:51 Jesus shocks us by announcing that the bread which gives life to the world is his own flesh, the flesh that he would offer as a sacrifice for all people, the flesh that he gives us to eat. He shocks us even more by declaring that we must not only eat his flesh but also drink his blood,[27] because his flesh is true food and his blood is true drink.

In this final part of his sermon Jesus draws the threads of his instruction together with a warning about rejecting that food and drink (6:53) and with four momentous promises about the benefits of the food and drink he supplies (6:54–58). He warns us that unless we actually eat his flesh and drink his blood we will not have his divine life in us. He assures us that if we feed on his flesh and drink his blood we will receive eternal life already, as a foretaste and pledge of our bodily resurrection; we will abide in him just as he abides in us;[28] we will receive life from God the living Father through Jesus; and we will live forever by feeding on the bread that God provides.

These words of Jesus make little sense unless we take them to refer to the Lord's Supper as the culmination of his earthly mission. They anticipate his establishment of that meal before his death and its ongoing celebration after his resurrection. In that meal he who had become flesh would give his flesh to his disciples for them to eat; he who had shed his blood for them would give them his blood to drink. There Jesus, the bread of life, would give them his flesh as "living bread," the bread that would ensure that those who ate it would never die but live forever (6:49–51). By feeding on him they would receive eternal life from the living, life-giving Father through him (6:57). By faith in him they would have eternal life (6:47, 54). The life that Jesus had would be in them and remain in them (6:53). Jesus would come to abide in them on earth, so that they could abide in him in heaven (6:56). In the Lord's Supper they would receive in this life a foretaste of the resurrection of their bodies for life with God in heaven (6:39, 44, 54). They would begin to live heavenly lives on earth.

Normally we assimilate the food that we eat. It becomes a part of us and our bodies. But in the Lord's Supper we have a food that assimilates us to itself. We become what we eat. We become like Jesus and share his divine life. His life-giving blood is transfused into us and remains in us. He transforms the biological life we have in our bodies into the spiritual life he has in his resurrected body, the life he has with his heavenly Father. Just as God gave his people life-sustaining food from heaven to feed them on their journey through the desert to the Promised Land, so he gives us the flesh and blood of Jesus as his life-giving food for us on our journey from earth to heaven. Our proper response to these amazing promises must surely be to join the crowd of people in the synagogue at Capernaum in praying, "Sir, give us this bread always" (6:34).

O living Bread from heaven,
How well you feed your guest!
The gifts that you have given
Have filled my heart with rest.
Oh, wondrous food of blessing,
Oh, cup that heals our woes!
My heart, this gift possessing,
With praises overflows.

My Lord, you here have led me
To this most holy place
And with yourself have fed me
The treasures of Your grace;
For you have freely given
What earth could never buy,
The bread of life from heaven,
That now I shall not die.

"O Living Bread from Heaven," verses 1–2
Johann Rist[29]

X

HOW CAN HE DO THIS?

How can this man give us his flesh to eat?
John 6:52 ESV

Imagine a sign on a billboard by the side of a road with nothing but the words: "Free food from J. Heavenly food for you." It is so plain that you would most likely ignore it until you began to be puzzled by it. Only then would you think about it and consider exactly what it was advertising. Was it really free? What kind of food was on offer, and for whom? Was it really heavenly food or just hype for an ordinary snack? Who was J., and where did J. offer this food? Was it available just once or as a permanent fixture? Whatever the case, its literal sense would seem too good to be true.

Jesus's sermon in the synagogue at Capernaum in John 6 is a bit like that. It puzzles us and yet entices us to consider something so wonderful that we think that it could not really be true, let alone literally true. It involves us because it is not a lecture but an odd dialogue between the congregation and Jesus, a discussion that raises question upon question as it unfolds—six in all! Even though Jesus does answer most of them (at least in part), he leaves the two most important, practical questions unanswered. How could he, a mere man, be the bread of life that had come down from heaven (6:42)? And how could a man give his flesh to eat for the life of the world (6:52)?

The topic of the sermon is quite clear. Jesus speaks about the imperishable food that he would provide for them. That's the hook that grips their attention, and ours too, as he leads his hearers deeper and deeper into a mystery—a mystery that becomes more mysterious as they are drawn into it, the mystery of Jesus as the bread of life, and the heavenly meal he would establish for his disciples. Yet he does not set out to bamboozle them but to whet their appetite for the best food of all, food that satisfies their spiritual hunger and thirst (6:35).

So let's ponder this mystery together by considering three things about the food we receive from him, and how we receive it. It is heavenly food that God the Father supplies for us; it is life-giving food that the risen Lord Jesus offers to people on earth; it is extraordinary food by which the Holy Spirit gives eternal life through what Jesus says and does by saying what he says.

The people Jesus had fed in the desert the previous day were puzzled by his disappearance from them, and now they asked him when he had come to the synagogue in Capernaum.

They asked that leading question because they wanted more food from him (6:26). They did not understand that this wonderful meal of perishable barley bread was not an end in itself but a sign of an even more wonderful meal of imperishable food that keeps on delivering eternal life. Jesus was able to provide this remarkable food because God the Father had commissioned him to do this on his behalf. Like the seal on a letter, the Father had put his seal, the seal of his Holy Spirit, on Jesus, the Son of Man, to consecrate and endorse him as his human agent who speaks and acts on his behalf. Thus God the Father gives Jesus as "the true bread from heaven," "the bread of God," "he who comes down from heaven and gives life to the world" (6:32–34). Just as the Father gives Jesus as the bread from heaven, so Jesus gives himself and his life to the world.

Jesus teaches the people in the synagogue about a divine, heavenly meal that God the Father has prepared for people on earth. It is a holy meal that Jesus hosts together with him. The Father also provides Jesus with the guests for it. Since the Father determines who joins Jesus and receives the bread of life he supplies, Jesus promises that he will never turn away any of those who come to him to be fed (6:37–39, 65). They are given to him by his Father to feed. People cannot come to Jesus unless the Father draws them to participate in his heavenly banquet (6:44). The Father also teaches them about Jesus and what they receive from him (6:45–46). All those who listen to the Father and believe what he says have eternal life. What's more, their faith in Jesus is a work of God, something produced by him and given to them (6:29).

Jesus teaches us that this wonderful meal with its life-giving menu is an integral part of God's purpose for Jesus as the Son of Man (6:27, 53, 62), the Holy One of God (6:69), the incarnate Son of God. He says this: "For I have come down from heaven, not to do my own will but the will of him who sent me. And this is the will of him who sent me, that I should lose nothing of all that he has given me, but raise it up on the last day. For this is the will of my Father, that everyone who looks on the Son and believes in him should have eternal life, and I will raise him up on the last day" (6:38–40).

I n and through Jesus God the Father gives the true bread from heaven to people on earth. They do not need to ascend into heaven to eat and drink in God's presence; they have hidden manna (Rev 2:17) already in their journey with him here on earth. Jesus emphasizes this by his repeated claim that the bread God provides has not just come down from heaven but is also still coming down from heaven. He himself had come down from heaven to earth as a man to do his Father's will (6:38, 41, 42). In fact, he himself was the living, life-giving bread that had come down from heaven (6:51, 58). Yet that would not end when his life on earth was over.

Jesus correlates his descent from the Father as God's Son with his ascent to the Father as the Son of Man (6:62). Both terms refer to Jesus as the human son of Joseph (6:42). While the former was offensive, the latter was even more offensive.

Since Jesus was a man with a human father and a human mother, how could he say that he had come down from heaven? Even worse, how could he give his flesh to eat for the life of the world? No human being, whether dead or alive, could ever do that, even if he were divinized by his ascent into the heavenly realm, like Enoch or Elijah. But Jesus was both the Son of Man (6:27, 53, 62) and the Son of God (6:40). He descended from his Father in heaven to take on a human body and ascended into heaven after his resurrection to take his human body and those who were joined bodily with him in flesh and blood as his brothers and sisters into his Father's presence (John 20:17). As the Son of God and the Son of Man he feeds his disciples with heavenly food on earth. He who shared their earthly, human life gives them his own heavenly, eternal life.

Jesus speaks about a meal that does not yet exist, a future meal, as if it were already available to his hearers (6:53–58). He uses the present tense to tell them about it and its amazing benefits. While his description scandalizes most of the crowd, it also whets the appetite of a few others. It is as if they have the menu and learn about its nutritional value without the actual meal. They would have to wait until the night before his sacrificial death, when he would establish this meal for them. Only then would his flesh be joined to some bread for them to eat physically, and his blood be joined to some wine for them to drink. They would have to wait until his resurrection and ascension for him to host this heavenly meal fully and regularly with them and others after them as a foretaste of their bodily resurrection and eternal life with God their Father in heaven. Only then would the descended and ascended Lord Jesus give himself as their food on their journey from earth to heaven.

The risen Lord Jesus shares his life with us in Holy Communion. By our participation in it we do not attain super biological vitality or gain superhuman power from him, so that we become supermen and superwomen with super brains and super bodies able to perform supernatural feats. He does not give us that kind of extraordinary earthly life. He gives us a different kind of life: heavenly life here on earth. We do not, like cannibals, eat the flesh of a dead person but the living flesh of the risen Lord Jesus. Unlike the "dead blood" that has been taken from an unknown person who has no contact with us, it is the living blood of the risen Lord Jesus that transfuses his life into us. As we eat his flesh and drink his blood, he shares his Holy Spirit with us physically in and through his flesh and blood, so that we have eternal life, spiritual vitality, his own divine life as God's Son. United with him, we share his life and become like him, even as we remain ourselves in every way. And that changes us gradually from the inside out. We become more and more spiritually alive as we feed on Jesus. We draw our life from him as we remain in him and he remains in us.

When many of his disciples were offended by his solemn assertion that they needed to eat his flesh and drink his blood, Jesus made this rather puzzling claim: "It is the Spirit who gives life; the flesh is no help at all. The words that I have spoken to you are spirit and life" (John 6:63). It is puzzling because he seems to contradict what he has just said about his flesh and the reception of eternal life by eating his flesh and drinking his blood. But that is not so at all. Rather he corrects their misunderstanding of what is meant by flesh and life.

In this response he distinguishes between normal human flesh that is kept alive by the air it breathes and his human flesh that gives life through the Holy Spirit that is in it. Human flesh remains alive only as long as it is animated by the breath of life in it; his flesh is filled with the Holy Spirit, who gives eternal life to those who are animated by him. Even though the flesh of a human being is alive, it is of no help when it comes to gaining and retaining eternal life. Only God can do that by his Holy Spirit and the bestowal of the Spirit by Jesus through his word.

Just as human words are formed and empowered by the air used to speak them, so Jesus gives his Spirit through the words he speaks, words that are inspired by the Holy Spirit and that inspire those who hear them. The Holy Spirit enlivens and empowers the words of Jesus so that they become "the words of eternal life" (6:68). Jesus speaks eternal life through his Spirit to those who hear him and believe in him. So those who believe what Jesus says about himself as the bread of life receive eternal life. His life-giving words convey the life-giving Holy Spirit through his flesh and blood to those who believe in them (6:64–68). Through faith in Jesus we therefore receive the spiritual blessings Jesus transmits from the Father to us as we feed on his living flesh and drink his living blood. Through faith in Jesus and his words we also know what it is that we receive from him in his Holy Supper. His words and his Spirit make it a heavenly feast for us on earth.

In the Lord's Supper the risen Lord Jesus, who has all authority in heaven and earth, performs an even greater miracle than when he fed five thousand people with five loaves and two fish, or walked across the lake at night to join his disciples in the boat. Since it is a miracle, it cannot be understood or explained in natural terms. In it Jesus works together with his heavenly Father and the Holy Spirit to give us eternal life. Through faith in him and what he says to us in the Supper we receive all that he offers to us there. He uses the human hands and mouths of his human ministers to deliver his body and blood to his disciples. We do not understand how this happens, but we do know that he does this in his Holy Supper. We know this by what he tells us. We know what he gives, and why. We know that he gives eternal life to us who believe in what he says and receive the consecrated bread and wine as his flesh and blood.

Unlike a billboard by the side of the road that advertises free food without any mention of what it is or where it is to be found, Jesus offers us heavenly food in the banquet he hosts for us on earth whenever and wherever we gather to eat his body and drink his blood. There he not only tells us what he dishes up for us, but also invites us to receive it as a free gift from him.

There he not only tells us how he gives it to us, but also how we are to receive it and its amazing benefits. There he shows us how his heavenly Father and the Holy Spirit work together with him to provide a heavenly feast for us here on earth.

O Bread of life from heaven,
To weary pilgrims given,
O Manna from above:
The souls that hunger feed Thou
The hearts that seek Thee lead Thou,
With Thy most sweet and tender love.

O Fount of grace redeeming,
O River ever streaming
From Jesus' holy side:
Come Thou, Thyself bestowing
On thirsting souls, and flowing
Till all their wants are satisfied.

Jesus, this feast receiving,
Thy Word of truth believing,
We Thee unseen adore:
Grant, when our race is ended,
That we, to heav'n ascended,
May see Thy glory evermore.

"O Bread of Life from Heaven"
Author unknown[30]

AND THAT WE
MAY EVERMORE DWELL
IN HIM AND
HE IN US

XI

HEAVEN ON EARTH

Therefore, brothers, since we have freedom of speech[31] for entrance into the holy places by the blood of Jesus, which he inaugurated for us as a new and living way through the curtain, that is, [the way] of his flesh, and [since we have] a great priest over the house of God, let us come near[32] with a true heart in the full assurance of faith, having had our hearts sprinkled from a bad conscience and having had our body washed with pure water.
Hebrews 10:19–22 (author's translation)

Access denied! Restricted access! Staff access only! No public access!

Such notices confront us all over the place, in computers and on documents, on buildings and at construction sites. They remind us that we do not always have access to all places. Access is often a matter of privilege rather than of right.

This applies most of all to people. Only my wife has access to me as her husband; only my children have access to me as their father, and to my home as their home. Access to people is always restricted. In fact, no one ever has the right of open access to another person. It is a privilege, something freely given which can never be taken for granted.

The letter to the Hebrews tells us that, amazingly, we have unrestricted access to God in worship through the flesh and blood of Jesus. Through faith in Jesus, our great high priest, we have the right of free speech with God, the freedom to approach him and address him in prayer to receive mercy from him and grace to help us when we need it (Heb 4:16). In the divine service or worship, we have the privilege of unrestricted access to God the Father and his grace through Jesus.

In the Old Testament only the high priest had access to God's hidden presence in the Holy of Holies, and that access was restricted to once a year on the Day of Atonement, when he would go through the curtain of the temple with the blood of the sin offering to sprinkle it on the mercy seat of the Ark of the Covenant. In the New Testament we have open access to God's presence in the heavenly sanctuary and its holy places through the flesh and blood of Jesus. This right of access is our inalienable endowment, part of our inheritance from God, a privilege that gives us confidence in our worship. It makes for assurance and certainty in our relationship with God and our approach of him.

The author of Hebrews gives us a glimpse of what is involved in this great privilege with its contrast between two mountains, earthly Sinai and heavenly Zion:

> For you have not come near to something that may be touched and to a blazing fire and to darkness and to gloom and to a storm cloud and to the blast of a horn and to a voice with utterances, whose hearers refused any further word that would be given to them because they could not bear what was commanded: "If even an animal touches the mountain, it must be stoned," and what was made visible was so frightful that Moses said, "I am terrified and trembling." But you have come near to Mount Zion and the city of the living God, heavenly Jerusalem, and to thousands of angels in festal gathering, and to the assembly of the firstborn who are enrolled in heaven, and to the Judge, who is God of all, and to the spirits of the righteous made perfect and to the mediator of a new covenant, Jesus, and to the blood for sprinkling that speaks something better than Abel. (Heb 12:18–24, author's translation)

Here the inaccessible presence of God in judgment on Mount Sinai is contrasted with the privilege of open access to God the gracious Judge and heavenly benefactor in heavenly Jerusalem. As we assemble to celebrate the Lord's Supper in that place, we have access to seven wonderful mysteries.[33]

I n Christian worship we assemble in two places at the same time. We gather as a congregation in an earthly place of worship. There is nothing very special about the place where we hear the word of God and receive his holy meal. Yet we also come to heavenly Jerusalem, the city of the living God, which is not located here on earth, even though we have access to it through Christ here on earth.

Solomon built his temple on Mount Zion in Jerusalem. There in the Holy of Holies heaven overlapped with earth. Only the high priest had access to God's heavenly presence there. But we do not gather there. When we come together for worship, we enter the city of the living God, the place where God the Father, the Son, and the Holy Spirit reside. This city is in this world, but it does not belong to this world. There we have access to the heavenly presence of God. There, by faith in Christ and his word, we enter the heavenly world without leaving this earth. There we join in the performance of the heavenly liturgy.

W e are not just surrounded by other human beings when we worship; we are surrounded on all sides by thousands and thousands of angels—more than we can count! The angels are God's heavenly servants. The writer of the Hebrews recalls Psalm 104:4 and calls them "liturgizing spirits," spirits in the divine service (Heb 1:14). Their main occupation is the performance of the heavenly liturgy, the worship of God with adoration, blessing, thanksgiving, and praise (Ps 29:1–2, 9; 103:20–21). They gather in festal assembly to praise and adore the risen Lord Jesus. They tell us of God's glory and his holiness. Amazingly, they invite us to join with them in their praises.

Since we, like them, are holy, we stand with them when we sing: "Glory to God in the highest" and "Holy, Holy, Holy." In fact, they act as a kind of spiritual choir for us; they assist us in our songs of thanksgiving and praise. They help us to adore and to glorify the Triune God. They share with us their wonder at the Father's grace and their joy at the Son's gift of peace. As we lift up our hearts and our spirits to the Lord, they carry us along and blend our song with their own. Thus we join the angels and archangels and all the company of heaven as we adore the living God in the eucharistic liturgy by singing or saying:

> Holy, holy, holy, Lord God of hosts;
> Heaven and earth are full of your glory;
> Hosanna in the highest!
> Blessed is he who comes in the name of the Lord;
> Hosanna in the highest!

Whenever we gather in the name of Jesus for worship on earth, we join a much larger supernatural assembly in heavenly Jerusalem (Matt 18:20). There we are part of a universal congregation that embraces our own congregation and every other congregation all over the world—for they all assemble, as we do, in the same place, the presence of the Triune God. So whenever and wherever we gather for worship in the name of Jesus, we gather with all believers everywhere. We worship together with them, no matter how far we may be from them in time and space. We join the whole church of God as it assembles in his holy presence.

As members of that assembly in heavenly Jerusalem we have a special status. On one hand, we are citizens of heaven. The Triune God is our divine king, and we have all the rights and privileges of citizenship in his royal city. We enjoy the life of heaven already here on earth. On the other hand, we have the status of God's firstborn Son, the same status as Jesus.

This is almost too good to be true. In the ancient world the firstborn son inherited the position and property of his father. Since Jesus is the firstborn Son of God, his only Son, he alone is God's heir. But he has wonderfully and generously shared his position and status with us in baptism: "You are my beloved Son; with you I am well pleased." Each of us, therefore, has the same status as Jesus, and we all stand to inherit everything that belongs to him.

But we don't have to wait until we die to enter our inheritance. In fact, by faith, we already begin to receive and enjoy our common spiritual inheritance, for unlike material possessions, which can be owned exclusively, spiritual blessings are always shared and held in common.

I n heavenly Jerusalem we meet with God the divine Judge, and there is no escape from his judgment when we gather for worship. Now that may scare off those of us with a guilty conscience. We know that we are not as we should be and have not lived as we should have. We fear God's accusation and condemnation more than anything. It's bad enough that we have to face God on judgment day. Who of us would wish to face God before we had to?

But God is present in our worship as a different kind of judge. He isn't out to disapprove of us, belittle us, and reject us as worthless and useless and ugly. No, he comes to free us from the burden of guilt and shame and to undo the awful aftermath of sin. He comes to pardon the evil we have done and to free us from evil that has been done to us. We have no reason to be afraid of contact with him. We don't have to wait until we die to discover where we stand with God. We can settle our accounts with him now, so that we need no longer fear his judgment and condemnation. We can welcome God's gracious judgment and receive his pardon now just as a sunny day in winter gives us a welcome foretaste of summer! We can receive the assurance of salvation from him. We can be sure of his approval and love for us now.

W e are like runners in a relay race. The Christians who have left this life have run in the race before us and have passed on the baton to us. Now they sit in the stadium and urge us on as we run our own lap in the race. They wait for us and the people who come after us to finish the race, so that they can celebrate together with us once the race is over. They have crossed the line, but we are still running.

Even though they are separated physically from us by death, they are still linked with us spiritually through the risen Lord Jesus. He keeps us in touch with them and them in touch with us. We can, therefore, more properly remember our loved ones at the Lord's Table than at the cemetery. They surround us, as Hebrews says, like "a cloud" (12:1), a cloud that conceals God's presence with us like the cloud of glory that accompanied God's people on their journey from Egypt to the Promised Land (Exod 13:21–22). They support us invisibly, just as all the other people who worship together with us do so visibly. Since we are connected with them in the communion of saints, they join us in the praise of the Triune God.

H eavenly worship centers on the risen Lord Jesus. He is the key to our involvement in it. Without him we remain earthbound and without access to the heavenly realm. He has bridged the great gap between heaven and earth for us by his death and resurrection. He is now our great high priest, our mediator with God the Father in the heavenly sanctuary. There he stands in for us with God the Father, even as he stands in for God the Father with us. He links us with all the angels, with Christians all over the world, with departed believers, and with our heavenly Father. Our extraordinary position depends on him and his work as our high priest. He gives us access to the heavenly realm and shares his holiness with us.

Jesus has set up a new covenant for us by the institution of Holy Communion: a new way of worship in which he gives us his body and blood. In this holy meal he reaches out to us on earth and joins us inseparably with himself. In the celebration of the divine service, which revolves around this sacrament, he acts as our high priest, our chief liturgist. Jesus not only brings the gifts of God the Father to us but also leads us in our prayers and praises.

We may therefore approach God the Father confidently through him—standing, as it were, in his shoes. In the divine service he comes to us, so that we can be with him in the presence of his heavenly Father. He brings heaven down to earth for us and takes us up from earth into the heavenly sanctuary, so that we stand with him and all the angels in the presence of his heavenly Father. He shares our life so that we can share in his divine life as God's Son.

T he heart of Christian worship is not just, as we might expect, the presence of the risen Lord Jesus. It also includes the gift of his holy and precious blood in his Holy

Supper, for only through his blood do we have access to heaven and the angels and the universal church and God the Judge and the faithful departed and the risen Lord Jesus.

In the Old Testament only the priests were allowed to approach God and officiate in the divine service of the temple. Before they could officiate, their bodies were sprinkled with blood at their ordination to the priesthood to cleanse them from impurity and to make them holy. Their right ears were smeared with the blood from the ram that was offered for their ordination so that they could hear the holy word of God; the thumbs of their right hands were smeared with blood, so that they could handle the holy things of God; the big toes of their right feet were smeared with blood, so that they could walk on holy ground (Exod 29:19–20; Lev 9:22–24). Then some of the blood that had been taken from the altar and mixed with the holy anointing oil was sprinkled on them and their vestments to consecrate them (Exod 29:21; Lev 8:30). In this way God shared his holiness with them. They could approach God only as long as they remained clean and holy.

In the heavenly Jerusalem we can go where no priest ever dared to go in the Old Testament. We can approach God the Father in the heavenly sanctuary and serve him there together with Jesus. Jesus has not just sprinkled our bodies with his blood; he sprinkles it on our hearts, our consciences, to purify us (Heb 8:12–14; 10:19–22) and make us completely holy (Heb 10:29; 13:12; see also 1 Thess 5:23). He sprinkles us by giving us his blood to drink in the Holy Supper. And that blood speaks something good to us. It doesn't speak of vengeance and banishment, as the blood of Abel did to his brother Cain who had murdered him. No—it speaks of grace and pardon and acceptance. By giving us his life-giving blood to drink, Jesus cleanses us entirely from the sins we have committed, as well as the sins that have been committed against us. Through his blood he shares his own purity and holiness with us. He makes us as holy as he is holy. His blood consecrates us as holy priests for service with the angels in the heavenly sanctuary. We can therefore approach God the Father boldly and unafraid, because we have been sprinkled with the blood of Jesus. We can bring others and their needs to our heavenly Father, even as we, mysteriously, bring him and his blessing to the people around us as we go about our daily work.

A ll this gives us boldness and confidence in our worship and our reception of Holy Communion. By the blood of Jesus we may approach God the Father with the full assurance of faith through the flesh of Jesus (Heb 10:19–22). Jesus is our high priest. He intercedes for us and leads us in worship. Our bodies have been cleansed by the waters of baptism and our consciences made holy with the blood of Jesus. We can enter the heavenly realm through the body and blood of Jesus. We can approach God the Father confidently without any doubts about our reception by him. We can be sure of his grace.

Wide open stand the gates adorned with pearl,
While round God's golden throne
The choirs of saints in endless circles curl,
And joyous praise the Son!
They watch him now, descending
To visit waiting earth.
The Lord of Life unending
Brings dying hope new birth!

He speaks the Word the bread and wine to bless:
"This is My flesh and blood!"
He bids us eat and drink with thankfulness
This gift of holy food.
All human thought must falter—
Our God stoops low to heal
Now present at the altar,
For us both host and meal!

The cherubim, their faces veiled from light,
While saints in wonder kneel,
Sing praise to Him whose face with glory bright
No earthly masks conceal.
This sacrament God gives us
Binds us in unity
Joins earth with heav'n beyond us,
Time with eternity!

"Wide Open Stand the Gates"
J. K. Loehe[34]

XII

FULL REMISSION

For this is My blood of the new covenant,
which is shed for many for the remission of sins.
Matthew 26:28 NKJV

Suppose you have been diagnosed with a severe case of blood cancer. The prognosis is grim. Unless it is arrested it will spread throughout your body and result in death. You undergo a radical course of treatment for it, and at its completion you visit your specialist to discover whether the treatment has been effective.

Then you receive the amazing news. The cancer is in remission. Not partial, temporary remission, but full, ongoing remission. You are free from it. The threat of sickness and death has gone. Your life and health have been restored.

Full remission! That's what Jesus provides for us by the blood he shed for us and now offers us in his Supper. He grants us full remission from the spiritual sickness of sin, the malignant cancer that infects us in our souls and bodies, for which there is no natural treatment or human remedy. The wages of sin—its outcome and cost—is always death (Rom 6:23).

Jesus reverses this by giving us his blood to drink in his Supper. Through it we have the eternal remission of all our sin. That is what I want to explore with you in this last chapter in a personal way. I want to meditate on the implication of that for me and for you.

But before I do that, I want to clarify how Jesus uses the Greek word for "remission."

It was commonly used as a secular, legal term to describe various kinds of release, such as the release from a debt, from a penalty for a crime, or from slavery. It was also used as a religious term in both the Old and New Testaments of the Bible to describe God's release of sinners from the debt of their transgressions against him. In that case their release occurred through the blood of an animal that had been sacrificed in atonement for them. Through the animal's blood they were not only released from the guilt of their sin, but also its toxic effects, its deadly consequences for them. By that release their relationships with God and with each other were restored. So when Jesus speaks of remission he does not just use it as a personal term for God's gracious attitude toward us, his unconditional acceptance of us despite the wrongs we have done, or as a legal term to describe God's merciful pardon for us as guilty people. It includes the positive outcome for us since we have been forgiven.

The remission of sins by the blood of Jesus has a widespread, far-reaching effect on us. It is a package that includes our release from a bad conscience, our release from the condemnation of the devil, our release from spiritual pollution, and our release from the threat of eternal death. All this is contained in the declaration in Hebrews 12:24 that the blood of Jesus sprinkled in our hearts speaks "a better word" than the blood of Abel. It does this in the Lord's Supper when Jesus himself says, "For this is My blood of the new covenant, which is shed for many for the remission of sins" (Matt 26:28 NKJV).

F or me the worst effect of sin is that it gives me a bad conscience, so that I don't just feel bad about the wrong things I have said and done; I feel bad about myself because I am not the person I should be. I may do what is right but my heart is not right with others and God.

And that puts me between a rock and a hard place. I make excuses and try to justify myself with God to restore my sense of worth and gain his approval. But the harder I try to be a good person, the more I realize my own personal failure. I don't fail occasionally but every day. If I have delusions about my own righteousness, the people around me remind me of my shortcomings. And God seems to make bad worse with his law and its demand to love him completely, and my neighbor as myself.

But amazingly, Jesus supplies me with the remedy for that. He lived and died and rose again to free me from the burden of a guilty conscience. He paid the penalty for my sin by his willing death for me. He rose again to justify me. He now gives me his blood to cover my sin and free me from my guilt. He frees me from the fear of divine disapproval. His blood reconciles me to him and brings me back into fellowship with his heavenly Father (Eph 2:13). As he gives me his blood to drink in his Holy Supper and sprinkles it on my conscience, he says to me, "Peace be with you! All your sins are forgiven; you are pardoned. My innocence and righteousness is yours. You have nothing to fear any longer. My heavenly Father is as pleased with you as he is with me. He loves you as much as he loves me."

I attend his Holy Supper to receive a good conscience from my heavenly Father. What could be better than that? It frees me from the chains of the past, the burden of present uncertainty, and the fear of the future. It frees me for the full enjoyment of all God's good gifts for me and all his faithful people.

E ven though I hear the blood of Jesus assure me that I am forgiven, I also often hear another voice within me, a voice in my heart that confuses and unsettles me, because it contradicts what Jesus says and discounts what he offers. Unlike the voice of Jesus that comes from outside me, it comes from deep within me and seems to be my own voice. I hear it most clearly when I meditate on God's word and attend the divine service. It sets off a conflict in my heart about me and my spiritual condition.

That inner voice confuses me because it uses God's law to show me how bad I am and how badly I have been wronged. It uses God's good law to attack my faith in him and my redemption by Jesus. It tries to convince me that I am unacceptable to God and rejected by him as unlovely and useless and worthless. And it does this so convincingly because I have failed him so often and don't measure up to his requirements for me as a Christian. I know that it does not come from me and my self-deception because it is the last thing I would ever want to say about myself. I also know that it does not come from God the Father and his Holy Spirit because it does not tell the full story about their plan for me as told in the Bible. It tells me that God the Father is not as pleased with me as he is with Jesus; it tells me that I am not righteous and holy, faultless and blameless, spotless and guiltless through faith in Jesus and his union with me.

Thus that voice is not the voice of God's Spirit but the voice of the evil spirit in me. He is called the devil because he slanders Jesus and us as Jesus's disciples. He is called Satan because he acts as if he is God, as if he has the right to accuse and condemn us. His voice in our hearts sets off a spiritual battle within us, the battle between him as our accuser and Jesus as our defender.

That spiritual battle is described most vividly in Revelation 12:1–17. It began with the ascension of Jesus into heaven and his expulsion of Satan and his rebellious angels from heaven to earth. There the devil now wages war against the members of the church who obey God's commandments and hold to its confession of faith in Jesus, the Lamb of God (12:17). Satan attacks them by accusing them of sin when they stand in God's presence (12:10). In this battle against Satan they have two spiritual weapons at their disposal: the blood of Jesus and their confession of faith in him. There they admit that they have sinned against him, but they win the victory against Satan by using his blood and their confession of faith in him to defy his accusation and reject his condemnation. They defeat him by receiving the blood in his Supper and relying on its application to them.

I therefore go to Holy Communion to overcome the condemnation of the devil. By my reception of Christ's blood and my reliance on it, I do not just get the devil off my back; I get him out of my heart. Even so his persistent voice is never completely silenced, because I continue to sin daily. But it loses its destructive power. Through the blood of Jesus that speaks the full remission of all my sins I can be sure there is now no condemnation for me.

My blood purifies my body from pollution and infection. It does not just bring oxygen from my lungs and nutrients from my intestines to each part of my body, but also absorbs the pollutants from it and brings them to my kidneys for removal. If my blood did not remove the toxins from my body they would gradually pollute and poison it, and I would die. My blood also distributes the antibodies produced elsewhere in my body to protect my organs from infection by attacking the germs that make me sick. My blood heals my body and maintains my physical health.

Paul Brand was a missionary doctor in India. When an epidemic of measles spread through the town where he lived, his daughter came down with a very bad case of it. Since he had no vaccine to treat her, Brand located a person who had recently recovered from measles. He drew blood from them and injected the plasma from their blood into his daughter. She was healed with blood that was borrowed from a person who had overcome the measles.

The apostle John tells us that the blood of Jesus does something far greater than that. He says in 1 John 1:7, "The blood of Jesus his Son cleanses us from all sin." When we sin we pollute ourselves. Sin contaminates us and our whole social order. It makes us unclean. And this does not just happen when we sin; it also happens when others sin against us. While we are not actually guilty of their sin, it still stains us; it taints our conscience just as our own sins do. We feel unclean and unwell, unworthy and unfit for God's presence. No matter how much we try, we can't cleanse ourselves from sin and its pervasive pollution. We all know this; we have all had some experience of an unclean conscience that makes us feel rotten about ourselves and unworthy of God.

Jesus gives me his blood to counteract that. His blood washes me clean inside; it gives me a clean, clear conscience (Heb 9:1–14). What a precious gift that is! His blood does not just remove my spiritual impurity; it also overcomes the sin that causes it. Remember Paul Brand's daughter. The blood of the person who had overcome measles overcame her measles by its transfusion into her. It is like that with Jesus. He took on all my sin by his life on earth with us and overcame every temptation I could ever suffer. He did this to produce the antidote to sin for me in my life on earth. He takes on all the wrongs I have done, as well as the wrongs that have been done against me, to give me his righteousness; he takes on my impurity to give me his purity; he takes on my spiritual sickness to give me his spiritual health. And he conveys all that to me by means of his blood in Holy Communion. There the blood of God's Son who overcame sin for us cleanses and heals me from the inside out. His blood saves me and makes me well again.

B lood sustains and maintains the life of every human being. The heart pumps it around to all parts of the body through the arteries and capillaries. It feeds every cell with nutrients and provides life-sustaining oxygen to muscle and tissue in the body. Blood gives life and supports life. Without blood there is no life. The loss of blood leads to weakness and death.

In his autobiography, Malcolm Muggeridge, a well-known English journalist and religious skeptic for much of his life, tells how he first began to understand what Christ accomplished by his death.[35] He was visiting a remote place with his wife. While they were there, she suffered such a severe haemorrhage that she was at the point of death. She needed a transfusion, but there was no blood bank there. When the doctor discovered that Muggeridge had the same blood type as his wife, he transfused Muggeridge's blood into his wife's veins. Muggeridge saved his wife's life by transfusing his own life-blood directly into her veins.

God's Son has done something far more wonderful than that. Even though he had created all life and was sustaining it with his powerful word (Heb 1:2–3; Col 1:15–17), he lived a human life to share his own divine life with us. He did not become a human being just to model the right way of life for us in human terms. No, he became a man for us to give us his own supernatural life, eternal life as the only Son of his heavenly Father, a share in the life of the Triune God—and that abundantly! And even more amazing, he does not convey his life to us genetically by becoming a father or mother to us. He does not convey his life mentally to us by teaching us about it. Rather, he conveys his life personally and orally to us in his Holy Supper. There he transfuses his own resurrected life into us as we drink his blood with the wine from the chalice. In John 6:53–54 he solemnly declares, "Truly, truly, I say to you, unless you eat the flesh of the Son of Man and drink his blood, you have no life in you. Whoever feeds on my flesh and drinks my blood has eternal life, and I will raise him up on the last day."

So then, drinking Christ's blood brings his life-giving Holy Spirit right into us who are otherwise spiritually dead in sin, even though we are physically alive. It gives us spiritual vitality and energy; it makes us more and more alive as we live in Christ and he lives in us; it gives life to our dying bodies and prepares them for the resurrection; it gives us a foretaste of the resurrection here and now in this earthly life. As we drink it we receive the Holy Spirit and share in the divine life of God.

The blood of Jesus releases me from the threat of eternal death. I am much like a person who suffers from hemophilia. Just as hemophiliacs need repeated blood transfusions to stay alive, so I need Christ's blood to keep me spiritually alive and active as I travel from earth to heaven. So I go to the Lord's Table to receive the life-blood of Jesus. Even though I can't see how it works, I take him at his word and trust in his blood to keep me spiritually alive. I rely on the blood of Jesus to sustain me as I pass through death to eternal life with God the Father. It prepares my dying body for its resurrection with Jesus. By it Jesus guarantees that my life won't end in death because he has "abolished death and brought life and immortality to light"

(2 Tim 1:10). What better word could the blood of Jesus speak to me than that?

I n the Lord's Supper Jesus gives us who trust in him his holy blood for the full remission of all our sins. This amazing gift includes all that he has won for us by his life and death, his resurrection and ascension. It is our inheritance from him, an inheritance based on the remission of sins and summed up in it. We do not just receive this inheritance from him when we die, but draw on it, like our pension, already in our life here on earth. But we draw on it without depleting it at all! In that holy meal we receive Jesus completely as our Savior, and with him everything that belongs to him as God's Son, everything that he has gained for us by his bodily life and death, as well as his bodily resurrection and ascension. All this is provided for us with his body and blood, given to us as a free gift for the remission of our sins.

Most amazingly, we receive all of this through faith in what Jesus says to us as his honored guests. His words are efficacious, performative words. They convey what they say; they grant what they pledge; they enact what they promise to do. They communicate the body and blood of the risen Lord Jesus audibly and physically to us through the bread we eat and wine we drink. Jesus says it, and gives what he says. So we believe what he says and receive what he gives as his heavenly gifts for our life here on earth.

What can wash away my stain?
Nothing but the blood of Jesus;
What can make me whole again?
Nothing but the blood of Jesus.
Oh precious is the flow
That makes me white as snow;
No other fount I know,
Nothing but the blood of Jesus.

For my cleansing this I see—
Nothing but the blood of Jesus;
For my pardon this my plea—
Nothing but the blood of Jesus.
Oh precious is the flow
That makes me white as snow.
No other fount I know,
Nothing but the blood of Jesus.

This is all my hope and peace—
Nothing but the blood of Jesus;
This is all my righteousness—
Nothing but the blood of Jesus.
Oh precious is the flow
That makes me white as snow.
No other fount I know,
Nothing but the blood of Jesus.

"Nothing but the Blood of Jesus," verses 1, 2, and 4
Robert Lowry[36]

AMEN

NOTES

The prayer beginning "We do not presume to come to this your table" on page xvii was drafted by Thomas Cranmer for the 1548 Anglican Order of Holy Communion.

NOTES ON THE MAIN TEXT

1. Didache 9:1, 5; Ignatius, *To the Philadelphians* 4:15; Ignatius, *To the Smyrnaeans* 8:1.
2. This subjective term seems now to refer rather vaguely to the friendly interaction of people with each other that results in a sense of community and communal solidarity.
3. See also the use of the verb for it with this sense in Romans 12:13 and Galatians 6:6.
4. See Oscar Cullmann, *Early Christian Worship* (London: SCM, 1953), 12–14.
5. Gerhard Wolter Molanus, "Your Table I Approach," trans. Matthias Loy, in *Lutheran Service Book* (St. Louis: Concordia, 2006), no. 628.
6. See Ezek 44:16; Mal 1:7, 12 for the designation of the altar for burnt offering as "the Lord's table."

7. The seven signs in John's Gospel are the transformation of water into wine (2:1–11), the healing of an official's dying son (4:46–54), the healing of a crippled man (5:1–8), the feeding of the five thousand (6:1–14), the walk of Jesus on the lake at night to join his disciples in their boat (6:16–21), the healing of a man who had been born blind (9:1–7), and the raising of Lazarus from death (11:38–44).

8. Charles Wesley, "Victim Divine, Your Grace We Claim," in *Lutheran Book of Worship* (St. Louis: Augsburg Fortress, 1978), 202.

9. See Luke 22:15–16, 17–22, 25–32, 34, 35a, 36–37, 38b. These mark the stages of his dialogue with his disciples during the meal. The second part of that conversation is interrupted by the report of what he said and did to inaugurate his new meal with them (22:19–20).

10. In the ancient world, kings were usually seated on a throne in the throne room of their palace when they acted in their royal capacity. On ceremonial occasions the king's courtiers were enthroned with him to show that they were authorized to administer his rule together with him. Likewise, judges and teachers sat on chairs when they operated in their official capacity. So, for example, in Matt 23:2 Jesus acknowledges that the scribes and Pharisees sat on the seat of Moses. Here Luke seems to combine all these functions for the apostles of Jesus. They serve as royal teachers and judges together with him.

11. Johann Franck, "Soul, Adorn Yourself with Gladness," trans. Catherine Winkworth, in *Evangelical Lutheran Hymnary* (St. Louis: Morningstar, 1996), 328.

12. The texts in table 1 are the author's own translation.

13. Horatius Bonar, "Here, O My Lord, I See Thee Face to Face," in *Lutheran Service Book* (St. Louis: Concordia, 2006), no. 631.

14. For use of this Greek verb to describe sacrificial self-offering see Matt 20:28; Mark 10:45; Gal 1:4; 1 Tim 2:6; Titus 2:14.

15. In Greek the same verb is used in all these instances. So "the night when he was betrayed" (1 Cor 11:23) was also the night before the day of divine sacrifice.

16. The significance of this will be explored and explained in the next chapter. In the sacrificial ritual of the old covenant a drink offering of wine was poured on the altar, but none of it was drunk by the priests or the people (Exod 29:40; Lev 10:8–11; Num 15:1–10).

17. Latin, 7th century, "Draw Near and Take the Body of the Lord," trans. John Mason Neale, in *Lutheran Service Book* (St. Louis: Concordia, 2006), no. 637.

18. See Matt 26:28; Mark 14:24; Luke 22:20; 1 Cor 11:25.

19. Thomas Aquinas, "Thee We Adore, O Hidden Savior," trans. James R. Woodford, in *Lutheran Service Book* (St. Louis: Concordia, 2006), no. 640.

20. Jesus does not just forgive the woman himself, but declares that she has been forgiven. This is a case of a divine passive, in which Jesus speaks a word of pardon and release from his heavenly Father.

21. It is telling that this incident occurs after Jesus's last prediction of his death in Luke 18:31–34 and on his journey through Jericho, on the way to his crucifixion in Jerusalem.

22. George Wallace Briggs, "Come, Risen Lord, and Deign to Be Our Guest," in *Together in Song* (Sydney: HarperCollins Religious, 1999), no. 524.

23. In Luke 22:11, Luke includes "given," which explains what is meant by "for you." He and Paul both use a preposition which means both "for you" and "on behalf of you."

24. James Montgomery, "According to Thy Gracious Word," in *Together in Song* (Sydney: HarperCollins Religious, 1999), 515.

25. In his Gospel John uses this term for the leaders of Israel who rejected Jesus out of hand and refused to believe in him.

26. Note that in John's Gospel Jesus did not just promise to give life, but claimed that he was the life (11:25).

27. There is nothing in the story of the manna in the desert and the feeding of the five thousand that prepares us for the unexpected mention of drinking blood here by Jesus, something that had been expressly forbidden by God.

28. See also John 15:4–5. Here Jesus uses *abide* to describe staying as a guest in the house of a host and residing there with him and his household. In the Lord's Supper Jesus comes to be at home in his disciples here on earth so that they may also be at home in him with his heavenly Father.

29. Johann Rist, "O Living Bread from Heaven," trans. Catherine Winkworth, in *Lutheran Service Book* (St. Louis: Concordia, 2006), no. 642.

30. Author unknown, 1661, "O Bread of Life from Heaven," trans. P. Schaff, in *Evangelical Lutheran Hymnary* (St. Louis: Morningstar, 1996), 266.

31. For a discussion of this Greek word, see the excursus on "The Privilege of Free Speech in Hebrews" in John W. Kleinig, *Hebrews* (St. Louis: Concordia, 2017), 171–75. The author of Hebrews uses it as a technical theological term for the right Jesus's disciples have to approach God's presence in his heavenly sanctuary freely and confidently to address him in worship and prayer (Heb 3:6; 4:16; 10:19, 35). We have this privilege of free speech through Jesus our great high priest.

32. For the use of this liturgical term in Hebrews see Kleinig, *Hebrews*, 226–29, 232–34.

33. For a fuller analysis this passage see Kleinig, *Hebrews*, 631–68.

34. J. K. Loehe, "Wide Open Stand the Gates," trans. Herman G. Stuempfle Jr., in *Lutheran Service Book* (St. Louis: Concordia, 2006), no. 639.

35. Malcolm Muggeridge, *Chronicles of Wasted Time, vol. 2, The Infernal Grove* (Glasgow: Fontana, 1975), 72.

36. Robert Lowry, "Nothing but the Blood of Jesus," in *Welcome Tidings: A New Collection of Sacred Songs for the Sunday School* (New York: Biglow & Main, 1877), 5.

SCRIPTURE INDEX

Old Testament

THE LORD'S SUPPER

The Christian Essentials series is
set in TEN OLDSTYLE, designed by
Robert Slimbach in 2017. This
typeface is inspired by Italian
humanist and Japanese
calligraphy, blending
energetic formality
with fanciful
elegance.

CHRISTIAN ESSENTIALS

*The Christian Essentials series passes
down tradition that matters. The ancient
church was founded on basic biblical
teachings and practices like the Ten
Commandments, baptism, the Apostles'
Creed, the Lord's Supper, the Lord's Prayer,
and corporate worship. These basics of the
Christian life have sustained and nurtured
every generation of the faithful—from
the apostles to today. The books in the
Christian Essentials series open up the
meaning of the foundations of our faith.*